Debbie Bliss

Teddy Bears

Twenty-five irresistible designs
for knitted bears

St. Martin's Griffin
New York

For my children, William and Eleanor

TEDDY BEARS. Text and designs © Debbie Bliss 1997. Photography copyright © Sandra Lane 1997. All rights reserved. Printed in Dubai. No part of this book may be used or reproduced in any manner whatsoever without written permission except in the case of brief quotations embodied in critical articles or reviews. For information, address St. Martin's Press, 175 Fifth Avenue, New York, NY 10010.

Library of Congress Cataloguing-in-Publication Data available on request.

First St. Martin's Griffin Edition: 1997
10 9 8 7 6 5 4 3 2

First published in the United Kingdom in 1997 by Ebury Press, Random House, 20 Vauxhall Bridge Road, London SW1V 2SA

Photography by Sandra Lane
Designed by Jerry Goldie Graphic Design
Styling by Marie Willey
Pattern checking by Tina Egleton

Printed and bound in Dubai / Oriental Press

ALSO BY DEBBIE BLISS
Toy Knits
New Baby Knits
Kid's Country Knits
Baby Knits
Kids' Knits for Heads, Hands and Toes
Nursery Knits

The author and publishers would like to thank the following for lending props for photography:

Old Town, 32 Elm Hill, Norwich
The Lacquer Chest, 75 Kensington Church Street, London

Contents

Introduction

Teddy Bears is a collection of 25 knitted bears, which I hope will appeal to bear-lovers everywhere. Appreciation of bears in not confined to age and there are teddies here that will have immense appeal for adults and children alike. There are bears to fit into small hands, a schoolboy bear in a uniform that can be knitted in the appropriate colour, and mascot bears for the fisherman, golfer or rugby player. I have done a trio of bedtime bears for cuddling up with, including a sleepy baby in a rabbit all-in-one and a number of different characters such as the Ballerina Bear, the French Bear or the Aviator Bear. Most of the bears have an interchangeable wardrobe of outfits, for example you can transform the rugged lumberjack into a stylish English gentleman in a tweed suit and the Edwardian in his old-fashioned swimsuit updates to a sporty jogger in a tracksuit.

     As with my other book of knitted toys, this book would not have been possible without the invaluable input of my children, Billy and Nell, and the technical assistance of Tina Egleton, my pattern checker.

Debbie Bliss

Basic Information

YARNS

All amounts are based on average requirements and should therefore be regarded as approximate. It is always best to use the yarn recommended in the knitting pattern instructions. Addresses for Rowan Yarns are given on page 80. If, however, you cannot find the yarn specified, you can substitute a yarn of similar weight and type. The descriptions of the various Rowan yarns are meant as a guide to the yarn weight and type (i.e. cotton, wool, et cetera). Remember that the description of the yarn weight is only a guide and you should test a yarn first to see if it will achieve the correct tensions (gauge).

The amount of substitute yarn needed is determined by the number of metres (yards) required rather than by the number of grammes (ounces). If you are unsure when choosing a suitable substitute, ask the assistant at your yarn shop to assist you.

Description of Rowan Yarns

Cotton Glace – a lightweight cotton yarn (100% cotton) approx 112m (123yd) per 50g (1¾oz) ball

Designer DK – a double knitting (US worsted) weight yarn (100% pure new wool) approx 115m (125yd) per 50g (1¾oz) ball

Handknit DK Cotton – a medium weight cotton yarn (100% cotton) approx 85m (90yd) per 50g (1¾oz) ball

True 4 ply Botany – a 4 ply yarn (100% pure new wool) approx 170m (220yd) per 50g (1¾oz) ball

Recycled – a chunky weight yarn (100% pure new wool) approx 100m (109yd) per 100g (3¾oz) hank

DK Tweed – a double knitting weight yarn (100% pure new wool) approx 110m (143yd) per 50g (1¾oz) hank

Lightweight DK – a lightweight double knitting weight yarn (100% pure new wool) approx 67.5m (75yd) per 25g (1oz) hank

Magpie Tweed – an Aran weight yarn (100% pure new wool) approx 150m (164yd) per 100g (3¾oz) hank

TENSION

Tension is the number of stitches and rows per centimetre (inch) that should be obtained on given needles, yarn and stitch pattern. To check your tension, knit a sample at least 12.5 x 12.5cm (5in) square, using the same yarn, needles and stitch pattern as those to be used for main work. Smooth out the finished sample on a flat surface but do not stretch it. With a ruler, mark out a 10cm (4in) square with pins. Count the number of stitches and rows between pins. If the number of stitches and rows is greater than specified try again using larger needles; if less use smaller needles.

Tension is not as crucial when knitting toys as it would be for other knitted garments. A tighter or looser tension will produce a smaller or larger toy than that shown in the photograph, and a loose tension will produce a more open fabric through which the stuffing will show or come through.

STUFFING

Overstuffing stretches the fabric so that the stuffing shows through and understuffing makes the toy too floppy. Watch out for 'lumps' when stuffing. Tear the edges of each piece of stuffing so that the edges blend in when inserted.

SAFETY

It is very important that a toy is suitable for the age of the child for whom it is intended. Toys given to children under 3 years of age should not have any added extras such as buttons or eyes which could become loose. Make sure that any toys given to the very young have all limbs and any accessories securely sewn in place. Washable stuffing, which conforms to safety standards, should always be used and yarns should be either 100% wool or 100% cotton.

ABBREVIATIONS

alt=alternate
beg=begin(ning)
cont=continue
dec=decreas(e)ing
foll=following
inc=increas(e)ing
k=knit
m1=make one by picking up loop lying between st just worked and next st and work into the back of it
patt=pattern
p=purl
psso=pass slipped stitch over
rem=remain(ing)
rep=repeat
sl=slip
skpo=slip 1, k1, pass slipped st over
st(s)=stitch(es)
st st=stocking stitch
tbl=through back of loop(s)
tog=together
yb=yarn back
yf=yarn forward
yon=yarn over needle
yrn=yarn round needle

6
Sleepy Bear in Rabbit Suit

SEE PAGE

33

Schoolboy Bear

SEE PAGE

37

Lumberjack Bear

SEE PAGE

41

Pyjama Bear with Dressing Gown

SEE PAGE

44

13
Golfing Bear

SEE PAGE

47

14
**Small Tweed Bear
in Jacket**
SEE PAGE
50

15
Tweed Bear in Duffel Coat

SEE PAGE

51

17
Edwardian Bear in Swimsuit

SEE PAGE

55

20/21
Aviator Bear
SEE PAGE

59

Fisherman Bear

SEE PAGE
64

24
Small Star Bear

SEE PAGE
67

Small Bear in Sweater

SEE PAGE

72

29
Ballerina Bear
SEE PAGE
75

Sleepy Bear in Rabbit Suit

See Page 6

MATERIALS
Bear 2 25g hanks of Rowan Lightweight DK.
Small amount of Brown yarn for embroidery.
Pair of $2\frac{3}{4}$mm (No 12/US 2) knitting needles.
Stuffing.
Rabbit suit 1 50g ball of Rowan True 4 ply Botany.
Pair of $3\frac{1}{4}$mm (No 10/US 3) knitting needles.
3 buttons.

MEASUREMENTS
Bear approximately 18cm/7in high.

TENSIONS
32 sts and 40 rows to 10cm/4in square over st st using Lightweight DK yarn and $2\frac{3}{4}$mm (No 12/US 2) needles.
28 sts and 36 rows to 10cm/4in square over st st using 4 ply yarn and $3\frac{1}{4}$mm (No 10/US 3) needles.

ABBREVIATIONS
See page 5.

Bear

LEGS (MAKE 2)
With $2\frac{3}{4}$mm (No 12/US 2) needles cast on 26 sts. Beg with a k row, work 5 rows in st st.
Next row P13, turn.
Work on this first set of sts only. Dec one st at beg of next row and foll alt row, then at end of foll row. 10 sts. Break off yarn and rejoin at inside edge to second set of 13 sts, p to end. Dec one st at end of next row and foll alt row, then at beg of foll row. 10 sts. K 1 row across both sets of sts. 20 sts. Work 10 rows.
Next row P10, turn.
Work on this set of sts only. Dec one st at each end of next 2 rows. 6 sts. Work 1 row. Cast off. Rejoin yarn to rem sts and complete as first side.

SOLES (MAKE 2)
With $2\frac{3}{4}$mm (No 12/US 2) needles cast on 3 sts. K 1 row. Cont in st st, inc one st at each end of next 2 rows and foll alt row. 9 sts. Work 6 rows straight. Dec one st at each end of next row and foll alt row, then on foll row. 3 sts. P 1 row. Cast off.

ARMS (MAKE 2)
* With $2\frac{3}{4}$mm (No 12/US 2) needles cast on 4 sts. Beg with a k row, work in st st, inc one st at each end of 3rd row and foll alt row. 8 sts. P 1 row.* Break off yarn. Work from * to *. K 1 row across both sets of sts. 16 sts. Inc one st at each end of 2nd row and foll 4th row. 20 sts. Work 9 rows straight.
Next row K10, turn.
Work on this set of sts only. Dec one st at each end of next 2 rows. 6 sts. Work 1 row. Cast off. Rejoin yarn to rem sts and complete as first side.

BODY (MAKE 2)
* With $2\frac{3}{4}$mm (No 12/US 2) needles cast on 3 sts. K 1 row. Cont in st st, inc one st at each end of next 2 rows and 2 foll alt rows. 11 sts.* Break off yarn. Work from * to *. P 1 row across both sets of sts. 22 sts. Work 12 rows straight. Dec one st at each end of next row and 2 foll 3rd rows, then on foll alt row. 14 sts. P1 row. Cast off.

BACK HEAD
With $2\frac{3}{4}$mm (No 12/US 2) needles cast on 3 sts. K 1 row. Cont in st st, inc one st at each end of next 2 rows, then at end of 3 foll rows. Work 1 row. Inc one st at beg of next row. 11 sts. K1 row. Break off yarn.
With $2\frac{3}{4}$mm (No 12/US 2) needles cast on 3 sts. K 1 row. Cont in st st, inc one st at each end of next 2 rows, then at beg of 3 foll rows. Work 1 row. Inc one st at end of next row. 11 sts. K 1 row. P 1 row across both sets of sts. 22 sts. Work 6 rows straight.
Next row K11, turn.
Work on this set of sts only. Dec one st at each end of next row. Work 1 row. Dec one st at end of next 3 rows. Mark end of last row. Dec one st at each end of next row. 4 sts. Work 1 row. Cast off.
Rejoin yarn at inside edge to rem sts and k to end. Dec one st at each end of next row. Work 1 row. Dec one st at beg of next 3 rows. Mark beg of last row. Dec one st at each end of next row. 4 sts. Work 1 row. Cast off.

RIGHT SIDE HEAD
With $2\frac{3}{4}$mm (No 12/US 2) needles cast on 6 sts. K 1 row. P 1 row, inc one st at beg. Cont in st st, inc one st at each end of next row, then at beg of foll 4 rows. Inc one st at end of next row and at beg of foll row. 15 sts. Work 5 rows straight. Mark end of last row. Cast off 2 sts at beg of next row. Dec one st at end of next row and at beg of foll row. * Dec one st at each end of next row and at beg of foll row.* Rep from * to *. 5 sts. Work 1 row. Mark beg of last row. Cast off.

LEFT SIDE HEAD
Work as given for Right Side Head, reversing shapings by reading p for k and k for p.

HEAD GUSSET
With $2\frac{3}{4}$mm (No 12/US 2) needles cast on 11 sts. Beg with a k row, work 4 rows in st st. Dec one st at each end of next row and foll alt row, then on foll row. Work 2 rows. Dec one st at each end of next row. Work 1 row. K3 tog and fasten off.

EARS (MAKE 4)
With $2\frac{3}{4}$mm (No 12/US 2) needles cast on 6 sts. Work 3 rows in st st. Dec one st at each end of next 2 rows. Cast off.

TO MAKE UP
Join instep, top and back leg seams, leaving an opening. Sew in soles. Stuff and close opening. Join arm seams, leaving an opening. Stuff and close opening. Join centre seam on each body piece. Join body pieces together, leaving cast off edge open. Stuff and gather open edge, pull up and secure. Join sides of head from cast on edge to first marker. Sew in head gusset, placing point at centre front seam and cast on edge in line with second marker on sides of head. Join centre seams of back head, then sew to front head, matching markers and leaving cast on edge open. Stuff and gather open edge, pull up and secure. Sew head to body. Attach yarn about 1cm/$\frac{1}{4}$in below top of one arm, thread yarn through body at shoulder position, then attach other arm, pull yarn tightly and thread through body again in same place, then attach yarn to first arm again and fasten off. Attach legs at hip position in same way as arms. Join paired ear pieces together and sew them in place. With Brown, embroider face features.

Rabbit Suit

LEFT LEG

With 3¼mm (No 10/US 3) needles cast on 35 sts. Beg with a k row, work 8 rows in st st.

Shape Instep

Next row K26, k2 tog, turn.

Next row Sl 1, p3, p2 tog, turn.

Next row Sl 1, k3, k2 tog, turn.

Next row Sl 1, p3, p2 tog, turn.

Next row Sl 1, k3, k2 tog, k to end.

Next row P9, p2 tog, p to end. 29 sts.

** next row K4, [k twice in next st, k6] 3 times, k twice in next st, k3. 33 sts.

Work 11 rows straight.

Shape Crotch

Dec one st at each end of next 2 rows. 29 sts.** Leave these sts on a spare needle.

RIGHT LEG

With 3¼mm (No 10/US 3) needles cast on 35 sts. Beg with a k row, work 8 rows in st st.

Shape Instep

Next row K12, k2 tog, turn.

Next row Sl 1, p3, p2 tog, turn.

Next row Sl 1, k3, k2 tog, turn.

Next row Sl 1, p3, p2 tog, turn.

Next row Sl 1, k3, k2 tog, k to end.

Next row P23, p2 tog, p to end. 29 sts.

Work as Left Leg from ** to **.

Next row K28, k last st tog with first st of Left Leg, k rem sts. 57 sts.

Work 3 rows straight.

Shape Front Opening

Cast off 3 sts at beg of next 2 rows. 51 sts. Work 10 rows straight.

Right Front

Next row K12, turn.

Work on this set of sts only for 5 rows.

Shape Neck

Cast off 2 sts at beg of next row. Dec one st at neck edge on next 3 rows. Work 3 rows straight. Cast off.

Back

Rejoin yarn to rem sts, k27, turn.

Work on this set of sts only for 9 rows.

Shape Neck

Next row K8, cast off next 11 sts, k to end.

Work on last set of 8 sts only. Dec one st at neck edge on next row. Work 1 row. Cast off.

Rejoin yarn to rem 8 sts and complete as first side.

Left Front

Rejoin yarn to rem sts and complete as Right Front, reversing neck shaping.

ARMS (MAKE 2)

With 3¼mm (No 10/US 3) needles cast on 28 sts. Beg with a k row, work in st st, dec one st at each end of 5th row and foll 4th row. 24 sts. Work 3 rows straight.

Next row K2 tog, k3, sl 1, k2 tog, psso, k8, sl 1, k2 tog, psso, k3, k2 tog.

P 1 row.

Next row K3, sl 1, k2 tog, psso, k6, sl 1, k2 tog, psso, k3.

P 1 row.

Next row K2, sl 1, k2 tog, psso, k4, sl 1, k2 tog, psso, k2.

Next row P1, p3 tog, p2, p3 tog, p1. Cast off.

SOLES (MAKE 2)

With 3¼mm (No 10/US 3) needles cast on 4 sts. Work in st st, inc one st at each end of 2nd row and foll next row, then on foll alt row. 10 sts. Work 7 rows straight. Dec one st at each end of next row and foll alt row, then on foll next row. 4 sts. Work 1 row. Cast off.

NECKBAND AND HOOD

Join shoulder seams.

With 3¼mm (No 10/US 3) needles and right side facing, k up 10 sts up right front neck, 3 sts down right back neck, 11 sts across centre back, 3 sts, up left back neck and 10 sts down left front neck. 37 sts.

1st rib row K1, [p1, k1] to end.

2nd rib row P1, [k1, p1] to end.

Rib 1 row more.

Next row Rib 4 and slip these 4 sts onto a safety pin, k5, [k twice in next st, k8] twice, k twice in next st, k5, turn, slip the last 4 sts onto safety pin. 32 sts.

Beg with a p row, work 15 rows in st st.

Next row K15, k2 tog, k4, k3 tog, turn.

Next row Sl 1, p9, p3 tog, turn.

*Next row Sl 1, k9, k2 tog, turn.

Next row Sl 1, p9, p2 tog, turn.*

Rep from * to * once.

** Next row Sl 1, k9, k3 tog, turn.

Next row Sl 1, p9, p3 tog, turn. **

Rep from * to * once, then from ** to ** once. Leave rem 13 sts on a needle.

With 3¼mm (No 10/US 3) needle and right side facing, sl 4 sts from right side of neckband onto needle, k up 11 sts along side of hood, k2 tog, k9, skpo across sts on needle, k up 11 sts down other side of hood, then rib the 4 sts on safety pin. 41 sts. Rib 2 rows. Cast off in rib.

BUTTONHOLE BAND

With 3¼mm (No 10/US 3) needles and right side facing, k up 20 sts along right edge of front opening to top of hood edging. Work 2 rows in p1, k1 rib.

Buttonhole row P1, k1, [yf, k2 tog, rib 4] 3 times.

Rib 2 rows. Cast off in rib.

BUTTON BAND

Work to match Buttonhole Band omitting buttonholes.

EARS (MAKE 2)

With 3¼mm (No 10/US 3) needles cast on 12 sts. K 40 rows.

Next row K2 tog, k to last 2 sts, skpo.

K3 rows. Rep last 4 rows until 2 sts rem. K2 tog and fasten off.

TO MAKE UP

Join leg, crotch and centre front seams. Sew in soles. Join arm seams, leaving cast on edge free. Sew in arms. Lap buttonhole band over button band and catch row end edges to base of opening. Sew on buttons. Pleat cast on edge of ears and secure, then sew them in place. Make a small pom-pon for tail and attach it in place.

Bear in Nightshirt with Hat

See Page
7

MATERIALS
Bear 3 25g hanks of Rowan Lightweight DK.
Small amount of Brown yarn for embroidery.
Pair of 2¾mm (No 12/US 2) knitting needles.
Stuffing.
Nightshirt, hat and slippers 1 50g ball of Rowan True 4 ply Botany in each of Cream (A), Light Blue (B) and Dark Blue (C).
Pair of 3¼mm (No 10/US 3) knitting needles.
3 buttons.

MEASUREMENTS
Bear approximately 27cm/10½in high.

TENSIONS
32 sts and 40 rows to 10cm/4in square over st st using Lightweight DK yarn and 2¾mm (No 12/US 2) needles.
28 sts and 36 rows to 10cm/4in square over st st using 4 ply yarn and 3¼mm (No 10/US 3) needles.

ABBREVIATIONS
See page 5.

Bear

LEGS (MAKE 2)
With 2¾mm (No 12/US 2) needles cast on 38 sts. Beg with a k row, work 8 rows in st st.
Next row K19, turn.
Work on this set of sts only. Dec one st at beg of next row and 2 foll alt rows, then at end of foll row. 15 sts. Work 2 rows. Break off yarn and rejoin at inside edge to second set of 19 sts, k to end. Dec one st at end of next row and 2 foll alt rows, then at beg of foll row. 15 sts. Work 2 rows. P 1 row across both set of sts. 30 sts. Work 14 rows.
Next row K15, turn.
Work on this set of sts only. Dec one st at each end of next 3 rows. 9 sts. Work 1 row. Cast off. Rejoin yarn to rem sts and complete as first side.

SOLE (MAKE 2)
With 2¾mm (No 12/US 2) needles cast on 4 sts. K 1 row. Cont in st st, inc one st at each end of next 2 rows and 2 foll alt rows. 12 sts. Work 9 rows straight. Dec one st at each end of next row and 2 foll alt rows, then on foll row. 4 sts. Work 1 row. Cast off.

ARMS (MAKE 2)
* With 2¾mm (No 12/US 2) needles cast on 7 sts. Beg with a k row, work 2 rows in st st. Cont in st st, inc one st at each end of next row and foll alt row. Work 1 row.* Inc one st at beg of next row. 12 sts. Work 1 row straight. Break off yarn. Rep from * to *. Inc one st at end of next row. 12 sts. Work 1 row. K 1 row across both set of sts. 24 sts. Inc one st at each end of 2nd row and 2 foll 6th rows. 30 sts. Work 11 rows straight.
Next row K15, turn.
Work on this set of sts only. Dec one st at each end of next 3 rows. 9 sts. Work 1 row. Cast off. Rejoin yarn to rem sts and complete as first side.

BODY (MAKE 2)
* With 2¾mm (No 12/US 2) needles cast on 5 sts. K 1 row. Cont in st st, inc one st at each end of next 2 rows and 3 foll alt rows. 15 sts. Work 1 row.* Break off yarn. Rep from * to *. K 1 row across both set of sts, inc one st at beg and end of this row. 32 sts. Work 19 rows straight. Dec one st at each end of next row and 2 foll 4th rows, then on 2 foll alt rows. 22 sts. Work 1 row. Cast off.

BACK HEAD
With 2¾mm (No 12/US 2) needles cast on 5 sts. K 1 row. Cont in st st, inc one st at each end of next 2 rows, then at beg of next 4 rows. Work 2 rows straight. Inc one st at beg of next 2 rows. 15 sts. Work 1 row. Break off yarn.
With 2¾mm (No 12/US 2) needles cast on 5 sts. K 1 row. Cont in st st, inc one st at each end of next 2 rows, then at end of foll 4 rows. Work 2 rows straight. Inc one st at end of next 2 rows. 15 sts. Work 1 row. K 1 row across both set of sts. 30 sts. Work 10 rows.
next row P15, turn.
Work on this set of sts only. Dec one st at each end of next row and foll 4th row, then on foll alt row. Dec one st at beg of next row. Mark beg of last row. Dec one st at each end of next row and at beg of foll row. 5 sts. Work 1 row. Cast off.
Rejoin yarn at inside edge to rem sts, p to end. Dec one st at each end of next row and foll 4th row, then on foll alt row. Dec one st at end of next row. Mark end of last row. Dec one st at each end of next row and at end of foll row. 5 sts. Work 1 row. Cast off.

RIGHT SIDE HEAD
With 2¾mm (No 12/US 2) needles cast on 8 sts. K 1 row. P 1 row inc one st at beg. Cont in st st, inc one st at each end of next row and at beg of foll 4 rows, then at end of next row and beg of foll row. Inc one st at each end of next row, then at beg of foll row and end of next row. 21 sts. Work 8 rows straight. Mark end of last row. Cast off 2 sts at beg of next row. Work 1 row. Dec one st at beg of next row and end of foll row. Dec one st at each end of next row, then at end of foll row, beg of next row and end of foll row. Dec one st at each end of next row and at end of foll row. Dec one st at each end of next row. 7 sts. Work 1 row. Mark beg of last row. Cast off.

LEFT SIDE HEAD
Work as given for Right Side Head, reversing shapings by reading p for k and k for p.

HEAD GUSSET
With 2¾mm (No 12/US 2) needles cast on 15 sts. Work 6 rows in st st. Dec one st at each end of next row and 3 foll 4th rows, then on foll alt row. Work 3 rows straight. Dec one st at each end of next row. Work 3 tog and fasten off.

EARS (MAKE 4)
With 2¾mm (No 12/US 2) needles cast on 9 sts. Work 4 rows in st st. Dec one st at each end of next row and foll alt row, then on foll row. 3 sts. Cast off.

TO MAKE UP
Join instep, top and back leg seams, leaving an opening. Sew in soles. Stuff and close opening. Join arm seams, leaving an opening. Stuff and close opening. Join centre seam of each body piece. Join body pieces together, leaving cast off edge open. Stuff and gather open edge, pull up and secure. Join sides of head from cast on edge to first marker. Sew in head gusset, placing point at centre front seam and cast on edge in line with second marker on sides of head. Join centre seams of back

head, then sew to front head, matching markers and leaving cast on edge open. Stuff and gather open edge, pull up and secure. Sew head to body. Attach yarn approximately 1cm/⅜in below top of one arm, thread yarn through body at shoulder position, then attach other arm, pull yarn tightly and thread through body again in same place, then attach yarn to first arm again and fasten off. Attach legs at hip position in same way as arms. Join paired ear pieces together and sew them in place. With Brown, embroider face features.

Nightshirt

BACK

Knitted sideways. With 3¼mm (No 10/US 3) needles and A, cast on 42 sts. Mark centre of cast on row. Beg with a k row, work in st st and stripe patt of 1 row B, 1 row A, 1 row B, 1 row C, 1 row B, 1 row A, 1 row B, 3 rows A throughout, work 12 rows.**

Shape Neck

Dec one st at beg of next row and at same edge on foll 2 rows. 39 sts. Patt 17 rows straight. Inc one st at each end of next row and at same edge on foll 2 rows. 42 sts. Patt 12 rows straight. Mark centre of last row. With A, cast off.

FRONT

Work as given for Back to **
Shape Neck

Cast off 4 sts at beg of next row. Dec one st at end of next row and at same edge on 4 foll rows.
Shape Opening

Cast off 16 sts at beg of next row. 17 sts. Patt 29 rows. Cast on 16 sts at beg of next row.
Shape Neck

Inc one st at end of next row and at same edge on 4 foll rows. Cast on 4 sts at beg of next row. 42 sts. Patt 12 rows straight. Mark centre of last row. With A, cast off.

SLEEVES

Join shoulder seams.
With 3¼mm (No 10/US 3) needles, A and right side facing, k up 44 sts between markers. Beg with a p row, work 2 rows in st st. Cont in st st and stripe patt as given for Back, dec one st at each end of 2nd row and 3 foll 4th rows, then on foll 3rd row. 34 sts. With A, k 3 rows. Cast off.

WELTS

With 3¼mm (No 10/US 3) needles, A and right side facing, k up 36 sts along lower edge of Back. K 2 rows. Cast off.
With 3¼mm (No 10/US 3) needles, A and right side facing, k up 50 sts along lower edge of Front. K 2 rows. Cast off.

NECKBAND

With 3¼mm (No 10/US 3) needles, A and right side facing, k up 12 sts up right front neck, 3 sts down right back neck, 13 sts across centre, 3 sts up left back neck and 12 sts down left front neck. 43 sts. K 4 rows. Cast off.

BUTTONHOLE BAND

With 3¼mm (No 10/US 3) needles and A, cast on 6 sts. K 8 rows.
Buttonhole row K2, k2 tog, yf, k2.
K 11 rows. Rep last 12 rows once more, then work the buttonhole row again. K 2 rows. Cast off.

BUTTON BAND

Work as given for Buttonhole Band omitting buttonholes.

TO MAKE UP

Join side and sleeve seams. Sew on bands and catch down cast on edge of button band to approximately 9 rows of base of opening. Form pleat with remaining rows and secure at top. Catch down cast on edge of buttonhole band to top of pleat. Sew on buttons.

Hat

TO MAKE

With 3¼mm (No 10/US 3) needles and A, cast on 72 sts. Work 16 rows in k1, p1 rib, inc one st at centre of last row. 73 sts. Beg with a k row, work 10 rows in st st.
Dec row K1, [k2 tog, k16] 4 times.
Work 3 rows straight.
Dec row K1, [k2 tog, k15] 4 times.
Work 3 rows.
Dec row K1, [k2 tog, k14] 4 times.
Cont in this way, dec 4 sts as set on every foll 4th row until 9 sts rem. Work 3 rows.
Dec row K1, [k2 tog] to end.
Break off yarn, thread end through rem sts, pull up and secure. Join seam, reversing seam on brim. Turn back brim. With B, make small pom-pon and attach to end of cap.

Slippers

TO MAKE

With 3¼mm (No 10/US 3) needles and B, cast on 4 sts for sole. K 1 row. Cont in st st, inc one st at each end of next 2 rows and 3 foll alt rows. 14 sts. Work 8 rows straight. Dec one st at each end of next row and 3 foll alt rows, then at each end of foll row. 4 sts. Work 1 row. Cast off.
With 3¼mm (No 10/US 3) needles and B, cast on 42 sts for top. Beg with a k row, work 8 rows in st st.
next row K24, k2 tog, turn.
next row Sl 1, p6, p2 tog, turn.
next row Sl 1, k6, k2 tog, turn.
Rep last 2 rows 3 times more, then work first of the 2 rows again.
next row Sl 1, k6, k2 tog, k to end.
next row K18, k2 tog, k to end. 30 sts.
K 1 row. Cast off knitwise. Join back seam. Sew in sole. With C, make a small pom-pon and attach to front of slipper. Make one more.

Schoolboy Bear

See Pages 8/9

MATERIALS
Bear 3 25g hanks of Rowan Lightweight DK.
Small amount of Brown yarn for embroidery.
Pair of $2\frac{3}{4}$mm (No 12/US 2) knitting needles.
Stuffing.
Outfit 2 25g hanks of Rowan Lightweight DK in Cream (A).
1 hank of same in each of Dark Grey (B), Light Grey (C) and Brown (D).
Small amount of same in each of Red (E) and Black (F).
Pair each of $2\frac{3}{4}$mm (No 12/US 2), $3\frac{1}{4}$ mm (No 10/US 3) and $3\frac{3}{4}$mm (No 9/US 4) knitting needles.
3 buttons. 2 press studs.
Length in each of narrow elastic and shirring elastic.

MEASUREMENTS
Bear approximately 27cm/$10\frac{1}{2}$in high.

TENSIONS
32 sts and 40 rows to 10cm/4in square over st st on $2\frac{3}{4}$mm (No 12/US 2) needles.
25 sts and 33 rows to 10cm/4in square over st st on $3\frac{3}{4}$mm (No 9/US 4) needles.

ABBREVIATIONS
See page 5.

Bear

LEGS (MAKE 2)
With $2\frac{3}{4}$mm (No 12/US 2) needles cast on 38 sts. Beg with a k row, work 8 rows in st st.
Next row K19, turn.
Work on this set of sts only. Dec one st at beg of next row and 2 foll alt rows, then at end of foll row. 15 sts. Work 2 rows. Break off yarn and rejoin at inside edge to second set of 19 sts, k to end. Dec one st at end of next row and 2 foll alt rows, then at beg of foll row. 15 sts. Work 2 rows. P 1 row across both set of sts. 30 sts. Work 14 rows.
Next row K15, turn.
Work on this set of sts only. Dec one st at each end of next 3 rows. 9 sts. Work 1 row. Cast off. Rejoin yarn to rem sts and complete as first side.

SOLE (MAKE 2)
With $2\frac{3}{4}$mm (No 12/US 2) needles cast on 4 sts. K 1 row. Cont in st st, inc one st at each end of next 2 rows and 2 foll alt rows. 12 sts. Work 9 rows straight. Dec one st at each end of next row and 2 foll alt rows, then on foll row. 4 sts. Work 1 row. Cast off.

ARMS (MAKE 2)
* With $2\frac{3}{4}$mm (No 12/US 2) needles cast on 7 sts. Beg with a k row, work 2 rows in st st. Cont in st st, inc one st at each end of next row and foll alt row. Work 1 row.* Inc one st at beg of next row. 12 sts. Work 1 row straight. Break off yarn. Rep from * to *. Inc one st at end of next row. 12 sts. Work 1 row. K 1 row across both set of sts. 24 sts. Inc one st at each end of 2nd row and 2 foll 6th rows. 30 sts. Work 11 rows straight.
Next row K15, turn.
Work on this set of sts only. Dec one st at each end of next 3 rows. 9 sts. Work 1 row. Cast off. Rejoin yarn to rem sts and complete as first side.

BODY (MAKE 2)
* With $2\frac{3}{4}$mm (No 12/US 2) needles cast on 5 sts. K 1 row. Cont in st st, inc one st at each end of next 2 rows and 3 foll alt rows. 15 sts. Work 1 row.* Break off yarn. Rep from * to *. K 1 row across both set of sts, inc one st at beg and end of this row. 32 sts. Work 19 rows straight. Dec one st at each end of next row and 2 foll 4th rows, then on 2 foll alt rows. 22 sts. Work 1 row. Cast off.

BACK HEAD
With $2\frac{3}{4}$mm (No 12/US 2) needles cast on 5 sts. K 1 row. Cont in st st, inc one st at each end of next 2 rows, then at beg of next 4 rows. Work 2 rows straight. Inc one st at beg of next 2 rows. 15 sts. Work 1 row. Break off yarn.
With $2\frac{3}{4}$mm (No 12/US 2) needles cast on 5 sts. K 1 row. Cont in st st, inc one st at each end of next 2 rows, then at end of foll 4 rows. Work 2 rows straight. Inc one st at end of next 2 rows. 15 sts. Work 1 row. K 1 row across both set of sts. 30 sts. Work 10 rows.
next row P15, turn.
Work on this set of sts only. Dec one st at each end of next row and foll 4th row, then on foll alt row. Dec one st at beg of next row. Mark beg of last row. Dec one st at each end of next row and at beg of foll row. 5 sts. Work 1 row. Cast off.
Rejoin yarn at inside edge to rem sts, p to end. Dec one st at each end of next row and foll 4th row, then on foll alt row. Dec one st at end of next row. Mark end of last row. Dec one st at each end of next row and at end of foll row. 5 sts. Work 1 row. Cast off.

RIGHT SIDE HEAD
With $2\frac{3}{4}$mm (No 12/US 2) needles cast on 8 sts. K 1 row. P 1 row inc one st at beg. Cont in st st, inc one st at each end of next row and at beg of foll 4 rows, then at end of next row and beg of foll row. Inc one st at each end of next row, then at beg of foll row and end of next row. 21 sts. Work 8 rows straight. Mark end of last row. Cast off 2 sts at beg of next row. Work 1 row. Dec one st at beg of next row and end of foll row. Dec one st at each end of next row, then at end of foll row, beg of next row and end of foll row. Dec one st at each end of next row and at end of foll row. Dec one st at each end of next row. 7 sts. Work 1 row. Mark beg of last row. Cast off.

LEFT SIDE HEAD
Work as given for Right Side Head, reversing shapings by reading p for k and k for p.

HEAD GUSSET
With $2\frac{3}{4}$mm (No 12/US 2) needles cast on 15 sts. Work 6 rows in st st. Dec one st at each end of next row and 3 foll 4th rows, then on foll alt row. Work 3 rows straight. Dec one st at each end of next row. Work 3 tog and fasten off.

EARS (MAKE 4)
With $2\frac{3}{4}$mm (No 12/US 2) needles cast on 9 sts. Work 4 rows in st st. Dec one st at each end of next row and foll alt row, then on foll row. 3 sts. Cast off.

TO MAKE UP
Join instep, top and back leg seams, leaving an opening. Sew in soles. Stuff and close opening. Join arm seams, leaving an opening. Stuff and close opening. Join centre seam of each body piece. Join body pieces together, leaving cast off edge open. Stuff and gather open edge, pull up and secure. Join sides of head from cast on edge to

first marker. Sew in head gusset, placing point at centre front seam and cast on edge in line with second marker on sides of head. Join centre seams of back head, then sew to front head, matching markers and leaving cast on edge open. Stuff and gather open edge, pull up and secure. Sew head to body. Attach yarn approximately 1cm/⅜in below top of one arm, thread yarn through body at shoulder position, then attach other arm, pull yarn tightly and thread through body again in same place, then attach yarn to first arm again and fasten off. Attach legs at hip position in same way as arms. Join paired ear pieces together and sew them in place. With Brown, embroider face features.

Shirt

BACK
With 3¾mm (No 9/US 4) needles and A, cast on 32 sts. Beg with a k row, work 14 rows in st st.
Shape Armholes
Cast off 2 sts at beg of next 2 rows. Dec one st at each end of next 2 rows. 24 sts. Work 12 rows straight.
Shape Neck
Next row K9, cast off 6 sts, k to end. Work on last set of sts only. Dec one st at neck edge on next 2 rows. 7 sts.

LEFT FRONT
Work 5 rows straight. Inc one st at neck edge on next 4 rows. Cast on 3 sts at beg of next row. 14 sts.
next row P12, k2.
Buttonhole row K2, yf, k2 tog, k to end. Keeping the 2 sts at front edge in garter st (every row k) and remainder in st st, work 7 rows. Inc one st at armhole edge of next 2 rows. Rep the buttonhole row. Cast on 2 sts at beg of next row. 18 sts. Work 14 rows straight, making buttonhole on 9th row. Cast off.

RIGHT FRONT
Rejoin yarn at inside edge to rem sts. Complete to match Left Front, omitting buttonholes.

SLEEVES
With 3¾mm (No 9/US 4) needles and A, cast on 27 sts. K 3 rows.
next row K1, [k twice in next st, k3] 6 times, k twice in next st, k1. 34 sts. Beg with a p row, work 13 rows in st st, inc one st at each end of 3rd row. 36 sts.
Shape Top
Cast off 2 sts at beg of next 2 rows. Dec one st at each end of next 2 rows. Cast off.

COLLAR
With 3¾mm (No 9/US 4) needles, A and right side facing, k up 35 sts around neck edge, omitting front borders.
Next row K.
Next row K2, p31, k2.
Rep last 2 rows twice more. K 3 rows. Cast off loosely.

TO MAKE UP
Join side and sleeve seams. Sew in sleeves. Sew on buttons.

Shorts

TO MAKE
With 3¾mm (No 9/US 4) needles and B, cast on 44 sts for leg. Beg with a k row, work 3 rows in st st, dec 2 sts evenly across last row. 42 sts. Beg with a k row (thus reversing fabric), work 8 rows in st st.
Shape Crotch
Cast off 2 sts at beg of next 2 rows. Dec one st at each end of next 2 rows. 34 sts. Work 16 rows straight. Work 4 rows in k1 p1 rib. Cast off in rib. Work one more.
Join centre back and front seams, then crotch and leg seams, reversing seams on cuffs. Turn back cuffs. Thread 2 rows of shirring elastic along wrong side of rib. Fasten off.

Slipover

BACK
With 3¾mm (No 9/US 4) needles and C, cast on 36 sts. Work 3 rows in k1, p1 rib, inc one st at centre of last row. 37 sts. Beg with a p row, work 9 rows in st st.
Shape Armholes
Cast off 3 sts at beg of next 2 rows. **
Dec one st at each end of next 3 rows. 25 sts. Work 17 rows straight.
Shape Neck
Next row K8, turn.
Work on this set of sts only. Dec one st at neck edge on next 2 rows. 6 sts. Cast off. With right side facing, slip centre 9 sts onto a holder, rejoin yarn to rem sts and k to end. Dec one st at neck edge on next 2 rows. 6 sts. Cast off.

FRONT
Work as given for Back to **. Dec one st at each end of next 2 rows.
Shape Neck
Next row K2 tog, k11, turn.
Work on this set of sts only. Dec one st at neck edge on 2nd row and 5 foll 3rd rows. 6 sts. Work 3 rows. Cast off. With right side facing, slip centre st onto a safety pin, rejoin yarn to rem sts, k to

last 2 sts, k2 tog. Dec one st at neck edge on 2nd row and 5 foll 3rd rows. 6 sts. Work 3 rows. Cast off.

NECKBAND
Join right shoulder seam.
With 3¾mm (No 9/US 4) needles, C and right side facing, k up 20 sts down left front neck, k centre front st, k up 20 sts up right front neck, 3 sts down right back neck, k centre back sts, k up 4 sts up left back neck. 57 sts.
Next row [K1, p1] 17 times, k2 tog, p1, skpo, [p1, k1] 9 times.
Next row [P1, k1] 8 times, p1, k2 tog, k1, skpo, p1, [k1, p1] 16 times.
Rib 1 more row, dec one st at each side of centre front st as before. Cast off in rib, dec as before.

ARMBANDS
Join left shoulder and neckband seam. With 3¾mm (No 9/US 4) needles, C and right side facing, k up 47 sts around armhole edge. Work 3 rows in k1, p1 rib, beg alt rows p1. Cast off in rib.

TO MAKE UP
Join side and armband seams.

Satchel

TO MAKE
With 2¾mm (No 12/US 2) needles and D, cast on 23 sts for front of main part. Beg with a k row, work 17 rows in st st. Cast off knitwise.
With 2¾mm (No 12/US 2) needles and D, cast on 23 sts for back of main part. Beg with a k row, work 17 rows in st st. Mark each end of last row. Work a further 9 rows. Dec one st at each end of next 2 rows. Cast off.
With 2¾mm (No 12/US 2) needles and D, cast on 4 sts for side of main part. Work 17 rows in st st. Mark each end of last row. Work 34 rows. Mark each end of last row. Work 17 rows. Cast off.
Placing cast on edge of back of main part along side between markers and cast on and cast off edges of side to markers on back, sew on side. Sew front to side, placing cast on edge between markers.
With 2¾mm (No 12/US 2) needles and D, cast on 17 sts for front pocket. Beg with a k row, work 9 rows in st st. Cast off knitwise.
With 2¾mm (No 12/US 2) needles and D, cast on 4 sts for side of pocket. Work 9 rows in st st. Mark one edge of last row. Work 25 rows. Mark same edge of last row as before. Work 9 rows. Cast off. Sew pocket to side, placing cast on edge between markers. Sew on pocket

in place.
With 2¾mm (No 12/US 2) needles and D, cast on 3 sts for small strap. K 13 rows. Cast off. Make one more. Sew on straps on fold of main part back. Sew tops of press studs to small straps, sew other end to pocket.
With 2¾mm (No 12/US 2) needles and D, cast on 50 sts for large strap. K 3 rows. Cast off. Make one more. Sew ends of large straps to back of satchel.

Tie

TO MAKE

With 3¼mm (No 10/US 3) needles and E, cast on 5 sts. K 5 rows, inc one st at each end of 2nd row and foll alt row. 9 sts.
Cont in garter st (every row k) and stripe patt of 2 rows F, 2 rows E, 2 rows F and 6 rows E throughout, work 10 rows. Dec one st at each end of next row and foll 6th row. 5 sts. Work 55 rows straight. Cast off.
Make a knot at centre of tie and secure in position. Thread length (to fit around bears neck under shirt collar) of narrow elastic throught top of the knot. Join ends of elastic.

Gardener Bear

See Page
10

MATERIALS

Bear 4 25g hanks of Rowan Lightweight DK in Brown (A).
Small amount of same in Black (B).
Pair of 2¾mm (No 12/US 2) knitting needles.
Stuffing.
Outfit 2 50g balls of Rowan True 4 ply Botany in Blue (C).
1 ball of same in Cream (D).
Small amount of same in Red (E).
Length of Silver lurex yarn.
Pair of 3¼mm (No 10/US 3) knitting needles.
3 buttons.

MEASUREMENTS

Bear approximately 32cm/12½in high.

TENSIONS

32 sts and 40 rows to 10cm/4in square over st st using Lightweight DK yarn and 2¾mm (No 12/US 2) needles.
28 sts and 36 rows to 10cm/4in square over st st using 4 ply yarn and 3¼mm (No 10/US 3) needles.
26 sts and 34 rows to 10cm/4in square over st st using 2 strands of 4 ply yarn together and 3¼mm (No 10/US 3) needles.

ABBREVIATIONS

See page 5.

Bear

RIGHT LEG

With 2¾mm (No 12/US 2) needles and A, cast on 24 sts. P 1 row.
Next row K1, [m1, k2] to last st, m1, k1. P 1 row.
Next row K9, [m1, k1] 3 times, [k1, m1] 3 times, k12, [m1, k1] 3 times, [k1, m1] 3 times, k3.
P 1 row.
Next row K12, [m1, k2] 4 times, k16, [m1, k2] 4 times, k4. 56 sts.
Work 13 rows in st st.
Next row K11, cast off next 12 sts, k to end.
Work across all sts.
Next row P30, p2 tog tbl, p2, p2 tog, p8.
Next row K7, k2 tog, k2, skpo, k16, skpo, k1, k2 tog, k8.
next row P7, p2 tog, p1, p2 tog tbl, p26. 36 sts.
** Work 6 rows. Inc one st at each end of next row and 2 foll 4th rows. 42 sts. Work 13 rows.
Next row K8, k2 tog, k1, skpo, k16, k2 tog, k1, skpo, k8.
Work 3 rows.
Next row K7, k2 tog, k1, skpo, k14, k2 tog, k1, skpo, k7.
Work 1 row.
Next row K6, k2 tog, k1, skpo, k12, k2 tog, k1, skpo, k6.
Work 1 row.
Next row K5, k2 tog, k1, skpo, k10, k2 tog, k1, skpo, k5.
Work 1 row.
Next row K4, k2 tog, k1, skpo, k8, k2 tog, k1, skpo, k4.
Next row P3, p2 tog tbl, p1, p2 tog, p6, p2 tog tbl, p1, p2 tog, p3.
Next row K2, k2 tog, k1, skpo, k4, k2 tog, k1, skpo, k2. 14 sts.
Cast off.

LEFT LEG

With 2¾mm (No 12/US 2) needles and A, cast on 24 sts. P 1 row.
Next row K1, [m1, k2] to last st, m1, k1. P 1 row.
Next row K3, [m1, k1] 3 times, [k1, m1] 3 times, k12, [m1, k1] 3 times, [k1, m1] 3 times, k9.
P 1 row.
Next row K6, [m1, k2] 4 times, k16, [m1, k2] 4 times, k10. 56 sts.
Work 13 rows in st st.
Next row K33, cast off next 12 sts, k to end.
Work across all sts.
Next row P8, p2 tog tbl, p2, p2 tog, p30.
Next row K8, skpo, k1, k2 tog, k16, k2 tog, k2, skpo, k7.
Next row P26, p2 tog, p1, p2 tog tbl, p7. 36 sts.
Complete as Right Leg from ** to end.

ARMS (MAKE 2)

With 2¾mm (No 12/US 2) needles and A, cast on 15 sts. P 1 row.
Next row K1, [m1, k2] to end. 22 sts.
Beg with a p row, work in st st, inc one st at each end of 4 foll alt rows, then on every foll 4th row until there are 40 sts.
Work 19 rows straight.
Next row K7, k2 tog, k2, skpo, k14, k2 tog, k2, skpo, k7.
Work 3 rows.
Next row K6, k2 tog, k2, skpo, k12, k2 tog, k2, skpo, k6.
Work 1 row.
Next row K5, k2 tog, k2, skpo, k10, k2 tog, k2, skpo, k5.
Work 1 row.
Next row K4, k2 tog, k2, skpo, k8, k2 tog, k2, skpo, k4.
Next row P3, p2 tog tbl, p2, p2 tog, p6, p2 tog tbl, p2, p2 tog, p3.
Next row K2, k2 tog, k2, skpo, k4, k2 tog, k2, skpo, k2. 16 sts.
Cast off.

BODY

Begin at neck edge.
With 2¾mm (No 12/US 2) needles and A, cast on 24 sts. P 1 row.
Next row K1, [m1, k2] to last st, m1, k1. P 1 row.
Next row K2, [m1, k3] to last st, m1, k1. 48 sts.

Work 7 rows in st st.
Next row K10, m1, k1, m1, k2, m1, k1, m1, k9, m1, k2, m1, k9, m1, k1, m1, k2, m1, k1, m1, k10.
Work 5 rows.
Next row K11, [m1, k2] 4 times, k9, m1, k2, m1, k11, [m1, k2] 4 times, k9.
P 1 row.
Next row K12, m1, k3, m1, k2, m1, k3, m1, k28, m1, k3, m1, k2, m1, k3, m1, k12. 76 sts.
Work 5 rows.
Next row K17, m1, k2, m1, k38, m1, k2, m1, k17.
Work 5 rows.
Next row K18, m1, k2, m1, k40, m1, k2, m1, k18.
Work 5 rows.
Next row K19, m1, k2, m1, k42, m1, k2, m1, k19. 88 sts.
Work 19 rows.
Next row K18, k2 tog, k2, skpo, k40, k2 tog, k2, skpo, k18.
P 1 row.
Next row K17, k2 tog, k2, skpo, k38, k2 tog, k2, skpo, k17.
P 1 row.
Next row K16, k2 tog, k2, skpo, k36, k2 tog, k2, skpo, k16.
P 1 row.
Next row K10, k2 tog, k3, k2 tog, k2, skpo, k3, skpo, k24, k2 tog, k3, k2 tog, k2, skpo, k3, skpo, k10.
P 1 row.
Next row K9, [k2 tog, k2] twice, [skpo, k2] twice, k6, skpo, k2, k2 tog, k8, [k2 tog, k2] twice, [skpo, k2] twice, k7.
P 1 row.
Next row K8, [k2 tog, k1] twice, [k1, skpo] twice, k6, skpo, k2, k2 tog, k6, [k2 tog, k1] twice, [k1, skpo] twice, k8.
P 1 row.
Next row K1, [k2 tog, k2] 3 times, [skpo, k2] 3 times, [k2 tog, k2] 3 times, [skpo, k2] twice, skpo, k1.
P 1 row.
Next row [K2 tog, k1] to end. 24 sts.
Cast off.

HEAD
Begin at neck edge,
With 2¾mm (No 12/US 2) needles and A, cast on 24 sts. Beg with a k row, work 4 rows in st st.
Next row K1, [m1, k2] to last st, m1, k1.
Work 3 rows.
Next row K2, [m1, k3] to last st, m1, k1.
Work 3 rows.
Next row Cast on 4, k7, [m1, k4] to last st, m1, k1.
Cast on 4 sts at beg of next 5 rows. 84 sts. Work 14 rows. Mark each end of last row. Cast off 9 sts at beg of next 2 rows. Dec one st at each end of next 5 rows, then on 3 foll alt rows. 50 sts. P 1 row.
Next row K18, [skpo, k2] twice, [k2 tog,

k2] twice, k3, skpo, turn.
Next row Sl 1, p20, p2 tog, turn.
Next row Sl 1, k20, skpo, turn.
Rep last 2 rows 3 times more, then work 1st of the 2 rows again.
next row Sl 1, k20, sl 1, k2 tog, psso, turn.
Next row Sl 1, p20, p3 tog, turn.
Next row Sl 1, k20, skpo, turn.
Next row Sl 1, p20, p2 tog, turn.
Rep last 2 rows 4 times more. Work on rem 22 sts for gusset. Dec one st at each end of 5th row and foll 4th row, then on 2 foll alt rows. P 1 row.
Next row K2 tog, k2, skpo, [k2, k2 tog] twice. 10 sts.
Work 7 rows. Dec one st at each end of every row until 2 sts rem. Work 2 tog and fasten off.

EARS (MAKE 4)
With 2¾mm (No 12/US 2) needles and A, cast on 20 sts. Work in st st, dec one st at each end of 7th row, foll 4th row, then on 2 foll alt rows. Dec one st at each end of next row. 10 sts. Cast off.

NOSE
With 2¾mm (No 12/US 2) needles and B, cast on 9 sts. Work in st st, dec one st at each end of 3rd row and 2 foll alt rows. Work 1 row. Work 3 tog and fasten off.

TO MAKE UP
Join instep, top and inner seams of legs, leaving cast on edge free. Stuff and join sole seams. Join top and underarm seams of arms, leaving an opening. Stuff and close opening. Fold sides of body to centre and join cast off edge together, then join back seam. Stuff and gather open edge, pull up and secure. Join underchin and snout seam of head from cast on edge to markers. Sew in gusset. Stuff and gather open edge, pull up and secure. Sew head to body.
Attach yarn approximately 1cm/¼in below top of one arm, thread through body at shoulder position, then attach other arm, pull up yarn tightly and thread through body again in same place, then attach yarn to first arm again and fasten off. Attach legs at hip position in same way as arms. Join paired ear pieces together and sew them in place. Sew on nose. With Black, embroider mouth and eyes.

Dungarees

RIGHT LEG
With 3¼mm (No 10/US 3) needles and using 2 strands of C yarn together, cast on 40 sts. K 3 rows.

Beg with a k row, work in st st, inc one st at each end of every 6th row until there are 56 sts. Work 2 rows. Mark each end of last row. Work 19 rows straight. **
Next row P9 and slip these sts onto a safety pin for back bib, cast off next 33 sts, p to end.
Leave rem 14 sts on a spare needle for front bib.

LEFT LEG
Work as Right Leg to **.
Next row P14 and slip these sts onto a spare needle for front bib, cast off next 33 sts, p to end.
Leave rem 9 sts on a safety pin for back bib.

BIB POCKET LINING
With 3¼mm (No 10/US 3) needles and using 2 strands of C yarn together, cast on 20 sts. Beg with a k row, work 17 rows in st st. Leave these sts on a holder.

FRONT BIB
With 3¼mm (No 10/US 3) needles, 2 strands of C yarn together and right side facing, rejoin yarn to Left Leg front bib sts, k to end, then k Right Leg front bib sts. 28 sts. K 3 rows.
1st row K to end.
2nd row K2, p24, k2.
Rep last 2 rows 7 times more.
Next row K4, cast off next 20 sts, k to end.
Next row K2, p2, p across sts of pocket lining, p2, k2.
Rep 1st and 2nd rows once. K 4 rows. Cast off.

BACK BIB
With 3¼mm (No 10/US 3) needles, 2 strands of C yarn together and right side facing, rejoin yarn to Right Leg back bib sts, k to end, then k Left Leg back bib sts. 18 sts.
1st row K2, p to last 2 sts, k2.
2nd row K.
3rd and 4th rows As 1st and 2nd rows.
5th row As 1st row.
6th row K2, skpo, k to last 4 sts, k2 tog, k2.
Rep last 6 rows twice more, then work 1st to 5th rows again.
Next row K1, skpo, k6, k2 tog, k1.
Next row K1, p3, k1, turn.
Work on this set of sts only.
Next row K5.
Next row K1, p3, k1.
Rep last 2 rows until strap, when slightly stretched, fits over Bears shoulder to top of front bib, ending with a k row. K 3 rows. Cast off.
With wrong side facing, rejoin yarn to rem sts, k1, p3, k1. Complete as first strap.

HANKIE
With 3¼mm (No 10/US 3) needles and E, cast on 19 sts. K 3 rows.
1st row K.
2nd row K2, p15, k2.
Rep last 2 rows 8 times more. K 3 rows. Cast off.

TO MAKE UP
Join leg seams to markers, then join centre back and front seams. Catch down pocket lining. Divide pocket in half with back stitch. Attach end of straps to front bib. Embroider buttons with lurex yarn. With Cream, embroider spots on hankie.

Shirt

FRONT
With 3¼mm (No 10/US 3) needles and D, cast on 44 sts. K5 rows.
Next row K.
next row K3, p38, k3.
Rep last 2 rows twice more. Cont in st st across all sts for 22 rows.
Divide for Opening
Next row K22, turn.
Work on this set of sts only.

Next row K3, p19.
Next row K.
Rep last 2 rows once more.
Buttonhole row K2 tog, yf, k1, p19.
Keeping border of 3 sts at inside edge as set, work 5 rows. Rep last 6 rows once more, then work the buttonhole row again.
Shape Neck
Next row K19 and turn; leave the 3 sts on a safety pin.
Dec one st at neck edge on next 3 rows, then on 4 foll alt rows. 12 sts. Work 5 rows straight. Break off yarn and rejoin at inside edge to second set of sts, k to end.
Next row P19, k3.
Next row K.
Rep last 2 rows 8 times more.
Shape Neck
Next row P19 and turn; leave the 3 sts on a safety pin.
Dec one st at neck edge on next 3 rows, then on 4 foll alt rows. 12 sts. Work 4 rows straight.
BACK
next row P12, cast on 20 sts, p across first set of sts. 44 sts.
Work 57 rows.
Next row K3, p38, k3.

Next row K.
Rep last 2 rows 6 times more. K 4 rows. Cast off.

SLEEVES
Place markers 30 rows down from shoulder at side edges of back and front.
With 3¼mm (No 10/US 3) needles, D and right side facing, k up 52 sts between markers.
Beg with a p row, work in st st, dec one st at each end of 5th row and every foll alt row until 34 sts rem. K 5 rows. Cast off.

NECKBAND
With 3¼mm (No 10/US 3) needles, D and right side facing, sl 3 sts from right front safety pin onto needle, k up 11 sts up right front neck, 18 sts across back neck and 11 sts down left front neck, then k3 sts from left front safety pin. 46 sts. K 4 rows. Cast off, dec first and last st.

TO MAKE UP
Join sleeve seams, then side seams to top of side edge borders. Sew on buttons.

Lumberjack Bear

See Page
11

MATERIALS
Bear 4 25g hanks of Rowan Lightweight DK.
Small amount of Brown yarn for embroidery.
Pair of 2¾mm (No 12/US 2) knitting needles.
Stuffing.
Outfit 2 50g balls of Rowan Designer DK Wool in Black (A).
1 ball of same in each of Red (B) and Dark Brown (C).
1 50g ball of Rowan True 4 ply Botany in Cream (D).
2 hanks of Rowan Lightweight DK in Beige (E).
Small amount of Rowan DK Tweed (F).
Oddment of DK yarn in Grey.
Pair each of 2¾mm (No 12/US 2), 3¼mm (No 10/US 3) and 4 mm (No 8/US 6) knitting needles.
Cable needle.
Small size crochet hook.
3 buttons for jacket and 3 buttons for shirt.
Small amount of stuffing.

MEASUREMENTS
Bear approximately 36cm/14in high.

TENSIONS
32 sts and 40 rows to 10cm/4in square over st st using Lightweight DK yarn and 2¾mm (No 12/US 2) needles.
24 sts and 32 rows to 10cm/4in square over st st using Designer DK yarn and 4mm (No 8/US 6) needles.
28 sts and 36 rows to 10cm/4in square over st st using 4 ply yarn and 3¼mm (No 10/US 3) needles.

ABBREVIATIONS
See page 5.

NOTES
Read chart from right to left on right side (k) rows and from left to right on wrong side (p) rows. When working colour pattern, strand yarn not in use loosely across wrong side to keep fabric elastic.

Bear

LEGS (MAKE 2)
With 2¾mm (No 12/US 2) needles cast on 50 sts. Beg with a k row, work 10 rows in st st.
Next row K25, turn.
Work on this set of sts only. Dec one st at beg of next row and 3 foll alt rows, then at end of next row and at beg of foll row. 19 sts. Work 1 row. Break off yarn and rejoin at inside edge to second set of 25 sts, k to end. Dec one st at end of next row and 3 foll alt rows, then at beg of next row and at end of foll row. 19 sts. Work 1 row. P 1 row across both set of sts. 38 sts. Work 21 rows.
Next row P19, turn.
Work on this set of sts only. Dec one st at each end of next row and 2 foll alt rows, then on 2 foll rows. 9 sts. Work 1 row. Cast off. Rejoin yarn to rem sts and complete as first side.

SOLE (MAKE 2)
With 2¾mm (No 12/US 2) needles cast

on 5 sts. K 1 row. Cont in st st, inc one st at each end of next 3 rows and foll alt row, then on foll 4th row. 15 sts. Work 11 rows straight. Dec one st at each end of next row, foll 4th row, and on foll alt row, then at each end of next 2 rows. 5 sts. Work 1 row. Cast off.

ARMS (MAKE 2)
* With 2¾mm (No 12/US 2) needles cast on 8 sts. Beg with a k row, work 2 rows in st st. Cont in st st, inc one st at each end of next row and foll alt row. Work 1 row.* Inc one st at beg of next row. Work 1 row. Inc one st at each end of foll row. 15 sts. Work 1 row. Break off yarn. Rep from * to *. Inc one st at end of next row. Work 1 row. Inc one st at each end of foll row. 15 sts. Work 1 row. K 1 row across both set of sts. 30 sts. Inc one st at each end of 2nd row and 3 foll 6th rows. 38 sts. Work 14 rows straight.
Next row P19, turn.
Work on this set of sts only. Dec one st at each end of next row and 2 foll alt rows, then on 2 foll rows. 9 sts. Work 1 row. Cast off. Rejoin yarn to rem sts and complete as first side.

BODY (MAKE 2)
* With 2¾mm (No 12/US 2) needles cast on 7 sts. K 1 row. Cont in st st, inc one st at each end of next 2 rows and 5 foll alt rows. 21 sts. Work 1 row.* Break off yarn. Rep from * to *. K 1 row across both set of sts. 42 sts. Work 25 rows straight. Dec one st at each end of next row, 2 foll 4th rows and 3 foll alt rows, then on every row until 20 sts rem. Work 1 row. Cast off.

BACK HEAD
With 2¾mm (No 12/US 2) needles cast on 7 sts. K 1 row. Cont in st st, inc one st at each end of next 2 rows, then at end of foll 5 rows. Work 1 row. Inc one st at beg of next 2 rows. 18 sts. Break off yarn.
With 2¾mm (No 12/US 2) needles cast on 7 sts. K 1 row. Cont in st st, inc one st at each end of next 2 rows, then at beg of foll 5 rows. Work 1 row. Inc one st at end of next 2 rows. 18 sts. P 1 row across both set of sts. 36 sts. Work 22 rows straight.
Next row K2 tog, k16, turn.
Work on this set of sts only. Dec one st at each end of 2 foll 3rd rows, then foll alt row. Mark beg of last row. Dec one st at end of next row, each end of foll row and at end of next row. 7 sts. Work 1 row. Cast off.
Rejoin yarn at inside edge to rem sts, k to last 2 sts, k2 tog. Dec one st at each end of 2 foll 3rd rows, then foll alt row. Mark end of last row. Dec one st at beg

of next row, each end of foll row and at beg of foll row. 7 sts. Work 1 row. Cast off.

RIGHT SIDE HEAD
With 2¾mm (No 12/US 2) needles cast on 10 sts. K 1 row. P 1 row inc one st at beg. Cont in st st, inc one st at each end of next row and at beg of foll 6 rows, then at end of next row. Inc one st at each end of next row. Inc one st at end of next row and at same edge on foll 3 rows. 26 sts. Work 11 rows straight. Mark end of last row. Cast off 2 sts at beg of next row. Dec one st at end of next row and at same edge on foll 6 rows. Dec one st at each end of next row, then at end of foll row. Dec one st at each end of foll alt row. Work 1 row. Dec one st at end of next 3 rows. 9 sts. Work 1 row. Mark end of last row. Cast off.

LEFT SIDE HEAD
Work as given for Right Side Head, reversing shapings by reading p for k and k for p.

HEAD GUSSET
With 2¾mm (No 12/US 2) needles cast on 20 sts. Work 10 rows in st st. Dec one st at each end of next row and 3 foll 4th rows, then on 3 foll alt rows. Work 3 rows. Dec one st at each end of next 2 rows. Work 2 tog and fasten off.

EARS (MAKE 4)
With 2¾mm (No 12/US 2) needles cast on 13 sts. Work 5 rows in st st. Dec one st at each end of next row and 2 foll alt rows, then on foll 2 rows. 3 sts. Cast off.

TO MAKE UP
Join instep, top and back leg seams, leaving an opening. Sew in soles. Stuff and close opening. Join arm seams, leaving an opening. Stuff and close opening. Join centre seam on each body piece. Join body pieces together, leaving cast off edge open. Stuff and gather open edge, pull up and secure. Join sides of head from cast on edge to first marker. Sew in head gusset, placing point at centre front seam and cast on edge in line with second markers on sides of head. Join centre seams of back head, then sew to front head, matching markers and leaving cast on edge open. Stuff and gather open edge, pull up and secure. Sew head to body. Attach yarn about 1cm/½in below top of one arm, thread yarn through body at shoulder position, then attach other arm, pull yarn tightly and thread through body again in same place, then attach yarn to first arm again and fasten off. Attach legs at hip position in same way as

arms. Join paired ear pieces together and sew them in place. With Brown, embroider face features.

Jacket

BACK
With 3¼mm (No 10/US 3) needles and B, cast on 44 sts. Beg with a k row, work 5 rows in st st. K 1 row for folding line. Change to 4 mm (No 8/US 6) needles. Beg with a k row, work in st st and patt from chart for 29 rows.
Shape Neck
Next row Patt 17, cast off next 10 sts, patt to end.
Work on last set of sts only. Dec one st at neck edge on next 3 rows. 14 sts. Cast off.
With right side facing, rejoin yarn to rem sts and complete as first side.

LEFT FRONT
With 3¼mm (No 10/US 3) needles and B, cast on 22 sts. Beg with a k row, work 5 rows in st st, inc one st at beg of 2nd row and at same edge on foll 2 rows. 25 sts. K 1 row for folding line.
Change to 4 mm (No 8/US 6) needles. Beg with a k row, work in st st and patt from chart for 23 rows.
Shape Neck
Cast off 6 sts at beg of next row. Dec one st at neck edge on next 5 rows. 14 sts. Work 4 rows straight. Cast off.

RIGHT FRONT
With 3¼mm (No 10/US 3) needles and B, cast on 22 sts. Beg with a k row, work 5 rows in st st, inc one st at end of 2nd row and at same edge on 2 foll rows. 25 sts. K 1 row for folding line.
Complete as given for Left Front, reversing shaping.

SLEEVES
With 3¼mm (No 10/US 3) needles and B, cast on 38 sts. Beg with a k row, work 5 rows in st st. K 1 row for folding line, inc 1 st at each end of row. 40 sts. Change to 4 mm (No 8/US 6) needles. Beg with a k row, work in st st and patt from chart, inc one st at each end of 3 foll 5th rows. 46 sts. Work 3 rows straight. Cast off.

COLLAR
Join shoulder seams.
With 3¼mm (No 10/US 3) needles, B, wrong side facing, and beg 4 sts in from front edge, k up 16 sts up left front neck, 20 sts around back neck and 16 sts down right front neck, ending 4 sts in from front edge. 52 sts. Beg with a p row, work in st st and patt from chart as

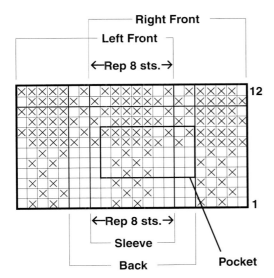

Right Front
Left Front
←Rep 8 sts.→

12

1

☒ = **Black (A)**
☐ = **Red (B)**

←Rep 8 sts.→
Sleeve
Back
Pocket

indicated for Back for 4 rows. Change to 4 mm (No 8/US 6) needles and patt a further 6 rows. Cont in A only. K 1 row for folding line.
Next row K3, [k2 tog, k5] to end. 45 sts.
Beg with a p row, work 5 rows in st st. Change to 3¼mm (No 10/US 3) needles and work a further 4 rows. Cast off.

FRONT FACINGS
With 3¼mm (No 10/US 3) needles, B and right side facing, k up 21 sts along left front edge. K 1 row for folding line. Beg with a k row, work 5 rows in st st, dec one st at beg of 2nd row and at same edge on foll 2 rows. 18 sts. Cast off.
Work right front facing to match.

POCKETS
With 4 mm (No 8/US 6) needles and B, cast on 9 sts. Beg with a k row, work in st st and patt from chart for 5 rows. With A, k 2 rows. Cast off. Work one more, reversing patt.

TO MAKE UP
Sew on sleeves, placing centre of sleeves to shoulder seams. Join side and sleeve seams. Fold all hems and facings at folding line to wrong side and slip stitch in place. Mitre corners and close openings at neck edge and at each end of collar. Sew on pockets and buttons. Make buttonholes by pushing large knitting needle through fabric.

Trousers

TO MAKE
With 4 mm (No 8/US 6) needles and C, cast on 40 sts for left leg. K 3 rows. Beg with a k row, work in st st, inc one st at

each end of 3rd row and 3 foll 6th rows. 48 sts. Work 3 rows straight.
Shape Crotch
Cast off 5 sts at beg of next 2 rows. 38 sts. Work 19 rows straight. ** K 4 rows.
*** **Next 2 rows** K4, sl 1, yf, turn, sl 1, k4.
Next 2 rows K3, sl 1, yf, turn, sl 1, k3.
Next 2 rows K2, sl 1, yf, turn, sl 1, k2. ***
K 1 row. Cast off.
Work right leg as given for left leg to **.
K3 rows. Work from *** to *** as given for left leg. K 2 rows. Cast off.
Join leg and crotch seams, then centre front and back seam.
With 4 mm (No 8/US 6) needles and A, cast on 86 sts for belt. K 4 rows. Cast off.
With 3¼mm (No 10/US 3) needles and Grey, cast on 7 sts for buckle. K 1 row.
Next row K2, cast off 3, k 1 st more.
Next row K2, cast on 3, k2.
K 1 row. Rep last 3 rows once more.
Cast off. Attach middle of buckle to one end of belt.

Shirt

Work as given for Shirt of Gardener Bear (see page 39).

Boots

TO MAKE
With 2¾mm (No 12/US 2) needles and E, cast on 62 sts for upper part. Beg with a k row, work 8 rows in st st. Dec one st at each end of next 3 rows.
Next row K1, k2 tog tbl, p50, k2 tog, k1. 54 sts.
Next row K
Next row K2, p50, k2.
Rep last 2 rows 6 times more. K 3 rows.

Cast off.
With 2¾mm (No 12/US 2) needles and E, cast on 24 sts for toe reinforcement. K 1 row.
1st row P20, yb, sl 1, yf, turn.
2nd row Sl 1, k16, yf, sl 1, yb, turn.
3rd row Sl 1, p13, yb, sl 1, yf, turn.
4th row Sl 1, k10, yf, sl 1, yb, turn.
5th row Sl 1, p7, yb, sl 1, yf, turn.
6th row Sl 1, k4, yf, sl 1, yb, turn.
7th row As 5th row.
8th row As 4th row.
9th row As 3rd row.
10th row As 2nd row.
11th row Sl 1, p20.
K 1 row across all sts. Rep 1st to 11th rows again. K 1 row across all sts. Cast off.
With 2¾mm (No 12/US 2) needles and using two strands of E yarn together, cast on 4 sts for sole. Work in st st, inc one st at each end of 2nd row and 2 foll rows, then 2 foll alt rows and foll 4th row. 16 sts. Work 8 rows straight. Dec one st at each end of next row, foll 4th row and 2 foll alt rows, then at each end of next 2 rows. 4 sts. Work 1 row. Cast off.
Join front seam of upper part to beg of garter st (every row k) border. Sew in sole. Fold toe reinforcement in half and join cast on and cast off edges together, stuffing widest part as you sew. Insert in boot and secure in place. With crochet hook and C, make chain approximately 41cm/16in long for lace. Lace boot. Make one more.

Hat

TO MAKE
With 4 mm (No 8/US 6) needles and A, cast on 19 sts for left side flap. Beg with a k row, work 11 rows in st st, inc one st at beg of 2nd row and at end of foll row. 21 sts. Leave these sts on a holder.
With 4 mm (No 8/US 6) needles and A, cast on 14 sts for peak. Beg with a k row, work 7 rows in st st, inc one st at each end of 2nd row and foll row. 18 sts. Leave these sts on a holder.
With 4 mm (No 8/US 6) needles and A, cast on 19 sts for right side flap. Beg with a k row, work 11 rows in st st, inc one st at end of 2nd row and at beg of foll row. 21 sts.
Next row P9, p2 tog, p10, p across peak sts, then p10, p2 tog, p9 across left side flap sts. 58 sts.
Beg with a k row, work 20 rows in st st. Cast off.
With 4 mm (No 8/US 6) needles and A, cast on 8 sts for crown. Work in st st, inc one st at each end of 2nd row and foll 2 rows, then on 2 foll alt rows and foll 4th row. 20 sts. Work 5 rows straight. Dec

one st at each end of next row and foll 4th row, 2 foll alt rows, then on next 2 rows. 8 sts. Work 1 row. Cast off.
With 4 mm (No 8/US 6) needles and A, cast on 5 sts for peak lining.
1st row (right side) K.
2nd row K winding yarn round needle twice for each st.
3rd row K dropping extra loops.
4th row Place cable needle in front of all loops of previous row, [pick up loop of corresponding st of first row and k tog with next st, thus enclosing cable

needle] to end. Pull out cable needle when you need to use it again.
These 4 rows form patt. Cont in patt, inc one st at end of next row and foll 4th row. 7 sts. Patt 43 rows more. Dec one st at end of next row and foll 4th row. Work 3 rows. Cast off.
With 4 mm (No 8/US 6) needles and A, cast on 7 sts for side flaps lining. Work in patt as given for peak lining, inc one st at end of 5th row and foll 4th row. 9 sts. Patt 143 rows more. Dec one st at end of next row and foll 4th row. Patt 3 rows. Cast off.

Join back seam of hat. Sew in crown. Sew on linings in place.

Sock Tops

TO MAKE
With 3¼mm (No 10/US 3) needles and F, cast on 50 sts. Work 10 rows in k1, p1 rib. Cast off in rib. Join back seam. Make one more.

Pyjama Bear with Dressing Gown

See Page *12*

MATERIALS
Bear 4 25g hanks of Rowan Lightweight DK.
Small amount of Brown yarn for embroidery.
Pair of 2¾mm (No 12/US 2) knitting needles.
Stuffing.
Pyjamas and slippers 1 50g ball of Rowan True 4 ply Botany in each of Dark Green (A), Red (B) and Light Green (C).
Pair of 3¼mm (No 10/US 3) knitting needles.
Small size crochet hook.
4 buttons.
Length of shirring elastic.
Dressing Gown 2 50g balls of Rowan True 4 ply Botany in Red (B).
Small amount of same in Green (A).

Pair of 3¼mm (No 10/US 3) knitting needles.
Small size crochet hook.

MEASUREMENTS
Bear approximately 36cm/14in high.

TENSIONS
32 sts and 40 rows to 10cm/4in square over st st using Lightweight DK yarn and 2¾mm (No 12/US 2) needles.
28 sts and 36 rows to 10cm/4in square over st st using 4 ply yarn and 3¼mm (No 10/US 3) needles.

ABBREVIATIONS
Dc = double crochet; ss = slip stitch.
Also see page 5.

Bear

LEGS (MAKE 2)
With 2¾mm (No 12/US 2) needles cast on 50 sts. Beg with a k row, work 10 rows in st st.
Next row K25, turn.
Work on this set of sts only. Dec one st at beg of next row and 3 foll alt rows, then at end of next row and at beg of foll row. 19 sts. Work 1 row. Break off yarn and rejoin at inside edge to second set of 25 sts, k to end. Dec one st at end of next row and 3 foll alt rows, then at beg of next row and at end of foll row. 19 sts. Work 1 row. P 1 row across both set of sts. 38 sts. Work 21 rows.
Next row P19, turn.

each end of next row and 2 foll alt rows, then on 2 foll rows. 9 sts. Work 1 row. Cast off. Rejoin yarn to rem sts and complete as first side.

SOLE (MAKE 2)
With 2¾mm (No 12/US 2) needles cast on 5 sts. K 1 row. Cont in st st, inc one st at each end of next 3 rows and foll alt row, then on foll 4th row. 15 sts. Work 11 rows straight. Dec one st at each end of next row, foll 4th row, and on foll alt row, then at each end of next 2 rows. 5 sts. Work 1 row. Cast off.

ARMS (MAKE 2)
* With 2¾mm (No 12/US 2) needles cast on 8 sts. Beg with a k row, work 2 rows in st st. Cont in st st, inc one st at each end of next row and foll alt row. Work 1

row.* Inc one st at beg of next row. Work 1 row. Inc one st at each end of foll row. 15 sts. Work 1 row. Break off yarn. Rep from * to *. Inc one st at end of next row. Work 1 row. Inc one st at each end of foll row. 15 sts. Work 1 row. K 1 row across both set of sts. 30 sts. Inc one st at each end of 2nd row and 3 foll 6th rows. 38 sts. Work 14 rows straight.
Next row P19, turn.
Work on this set of sts only. Dec one st at each end of next row and 2 foll alt rows, then on 2 foll rows. 9 sts. Work 1 row. Cast off. Rejoin yarn to rem sts and complete as first side.

BODY (MAKE 2)
* With 2¾mm (No 12/US 2) needles cast on 7 sts. K 1 row. Cont in st st, inc one st at each end of next 2 rows and 5 foll alt rows. 21 sts. Work 1 row.* Break off yarn. Rep from * to *. K 1 row across both set of sts. 42 sts. Work 25 rows straight. Dec one st at each end of next row, 2 foll 4th rows and 3 foll alt rows, then on every row until 20 sts rem. Work 1 row. Cast off.

BACK HEAD
With 2¾mm (No 12/US 2) needles cast on 7 sts. K 1 row. Cont in st st, inc one st at each end of next 2 rows, then at end of foll 5 rows. Work 1 row. Inc one st at beg of next 2 rows. 18 sts. Break off yarn.
With 2¾mm (No 12/US 2) needles cast on 7 sts. K 1 row. Cont in st st, inc one st at each end of next 2 rows, then at beg of foll 5 rows. Work 1 row. Inc one st at end of next 2 rows. 18 sts. P 1 row across both set of sts. 36 sts. Work 22 rows straight.
Next row K2 tog, k16, turn.
Work on this set of sts only. Dec one st at each end of 2 foll 3rd rows, then foll alt row. Mark beg of last row. Dec one st at end of next row, each end of foll row and

at end of next row. 7 sts. Work 1 row. Cast off.

Rejoin yarn at inside edge to rem sts, k to last 2 sts, k2 tog. Dec one st at each end of 2 foll 3rd rows, then foll alt row. Mark end of last row. Dec one st at beg of next row, each end of foll row and at beg of foll row. 7 sts. Work 1 row. Cast off.

RIGHT SIDE HEAD

With 2¾mm (No 12/US 2) needles cast on 10 sts. K 1 row. P 1 row inc one st at beg. Cont in st st, inc one st at each end of next row and at beg of foll 6 rows, then at end of next row. Inc one st at each end of next row. Inc one st at end of next row and at same edge on foll 3 rows. 26 sts. Work 11 rows straight. Mark end of last row. Cast off 2 sts at beg of next row. Dec one st at end of next row and at same edge on foll 6 rows. Dec one st at each end of next row, then at end of foll row. Dec one st at each end of foll alt row. Work 1 row. Dec one st at end of next 3 rows. 9 sts. Work 1 row. Mark end of last row. Cast off.

LEFT SIDE HEAD

Work as given for Right Side Head, reversing shapings by reading p for k and k for p.

HEAD GUSSET

With 2¾mm (No 12/US 2) needles cast on 20 sts. Work 10 rows in st st. Dec one st at each end of next row and 3 foll 4th rows, then on 3 foll alt rows. Work 3 rows. Dec one st at each end of next 2 rows. Work 2 tog and fasten off.

EARS (MAKE 4)

With 2¾mm (No 12/US 2) needles cast on 13 sts. Work 5 rows in st st. Dec one st at each end of next row and 2 foll alt rows, then on foll 2 rows. 3 sts. Cast off.

TO MAKE UP

Join instep, top and back leg seams, leaving an opening. Sew in soles. Stuff and close opening. Join arm seams, leaving an opening. Stuff and close opening. Join centre seam on each body piece. Join body pieces together, leaving cast off edge open. Stuff and gather open edge, pull up and secure. Join sides of head from cast on edge to first marker. Sew in head gusset, placing point at centre front seam and cast on edge in line with second markers on sides of head. Join centre seams of back head, then sew to front head, matching markers and leaving cast on edge open. Stuff and gather open edge, pull up and secure. Sew head to body. Attach yarn about 1cm/½in below top of one arm,

thread yarn through body at shoulder position, then attach other arm, pull yarn tightly and thread through body again in same place, then attach yarn to first arm again and fasten off. Attach legs at hip position in same way as arms. Join paired ear pieces together and sew them in place. With Brown, embroider face features.

Pyjama Top

BACK

With 3¼mm (No 10/US 3) needles and A, cast on 43 sts. K 3 rows. Beg with a k row, work in st st and stripe patt of 1 row B, 1 row A, 1 row C, 1 row A, 1 row B, 8 rows A until 25 rows have been worked.

Shape Armholes

Cast off 3 sts at beg of next 2 rows. Dec one st at each of next 4 rows. 29 sts. Patt 13 rows straight.

Shape Neck

Next row K9, cast off next 11 sts, k to end.

Work on last set of sts only. Dec one st at neck edge on next 2 rows. 7 sts. Work 1 row. Cast off.

Rejoin yarn at inside edge to rem sts and complete as first side.

LEFT FRONT

With 3¼mm (No 10/US 3) needles and A, cast on 20 sts. K3 rows. Work as given for Back until 24 rows have been worked.

Shape Neck and Armhole

Dec one st at end of next row. Work 1 row. Cast off 3 sts at beg of next row. Dec one st at armhole edge on next 4 rows, **at the same time,** dec one st at neck edge on foll 2nd row. 11 sts. Dec one st at neck edge only on 2nd row and 3 foll 4th rows. 7 sts. Work 3 rows straight. Cast off.

RIGHT FRONT

Work as given for Left Front, reversing shapings.

SLEEVES

With 3¼mm (No 10/US 3) needles and A, cast on 37 sts. K 3 rows.

Beg with a k row, work in st st and stripe patt as given for Back, inc one st at each end of 5th row and 2 foll 6th rows. 43 sts. Work 8 rows straight.

Shape Top

Cast off 3 sts at beg of next 2 rows and 5 sts at beg of foll 4 rows. Cast off rem sts.

BUTTONHOLE BAND AND LAPEL

With 3¼mm (No 10/US 3) needles and A, cast on 5 sts. K 5 rows.

Buttonhole row K1, k2 tog, yf, k2.

K 9 rows. Rep last 10 rows twice more,

then work the buttonhole row again. Cont in garter st (every row k), inc one st at beg of 4th row and 6 foll alt rows. 12 sts. K 3 rows. Cast off.

BUTTON BAND AND LAPEL

Work as given for Buttonhole Band and Lapel omitting buttonholes and reversing shaping.

COLLAR

With 3¼mm (No 10/US 3) needles and A, cast on 16 sts. Work 2 rows in garter st. Cast on 5 sts at beg of next 6 rows. 46 sts. Work 8 rows straight. Cast off.

POCKETS (MAKE 2)

With 3¼mm (No 10/US 3) needles and A, cast on 9 sts. Beg with a k row, work 7 rows in st st. Cast off knitwise.

TO MAKE UP

With crochet hook, right side facing and beginning above garter st edging between 3rd and 4th sts from side edge of back, *work vertical line in chain st with B, miss one st and work vertical line in C, then miss next st and work vertical line in B, miss next 5 sts. Rep from * to end of back. Work vertical lines on fronts, beginning from side edges. Beginning between 1st and 2nd sts and with C, work vertical lines on sleeves. Join shoulder, side and sleeve seams. Sew in sleeves. Sew on bands and lapels. Beginning and ending at centre of cast off edge of lapels, sew on collar. Place pockets on fronts and mark position of vertical lines. Work the lines, then sew on pockets. Sew on buttons.

Pyjama Bottom

TO MAKE

With 3¼mm (No 10/US 3) needles and A, cast on 58 sts. K 3 rows. Beg with a k row, work in st st and stripe pattern as given for Back of Pyjama Top until 25 rows have been worked.

Shape Crotch

Cast off 3 sts at beg of next 2 rows. Dec one st at each end of next 4 rows. 44 sts. Patt 27 rows. With A, work 5 rows in k1, p1 rib. Cast off in rib.

Make one more piece in same way. Work vertical lines in same way as given for Back of Pyjama Top. Join leg seams from cast on edge to beginning of crotch shaping, then join centre front and back seam. Thread shirring elastic along wrong side of rib and secure.

Slippers

TO MAKE

With 3¼mm (No 10/US 3) needles and B, cast on 51 sts for upper part. Beg with a k row, work in st st and stripe patt of 4 rows B, 1 row A, 1 row B, 1 row C, 1 row B, 1 row A, 4 rows B throughout, work 12 rows.

Next row K28, skpo, turn.
Next row Sl 1, p6, p2 tog, turn.
Next row Sl 1, k6, skpo, turn.
Rep last 2 rows once. K or p the sl st, rep last 2 rows twice more, then work first of the 2 rows again. Cont in B only.
Next row K7, k2 tog, k to end.
Next row K23, k2 tog, k to end.
K 1 row. Cast off knitwise. Beginning at cast on edge and using A instead of B, work vertical lines as given for Back of Pyjama Top, omitting top edging.
With 3¼mm (No 10/US 3) needles and B, cast on 5 sts for sole. Work in st st, inc one st at each end of 2nd row and 2 foll rows, then 2 foll alt rows and foll 4th row. 17 sts. Work 11 rows straight. Dec one st at each end of next row, foll 4th row and 2 foll alt rows, then at each end of next 2 rows. 5 sts. Work 1 row. Cast off. Join back seam of upper part. Sew in sole. Using all colours, make pom-pon and attach to front of slipper. Make one more.

Dressing Gown

BACK

With 3¼mm (No 10/US 3) needles and B, cast on 56 sts. Beg with a k row, work 40 rows in st st. Mark each end of last row. Work 29 rows.
Shape Neck
Next row P18, cast off next 20 sts, p to end.
Work on last set of sts only. Dec one st at neck edge on next 4 rows. 14 sts. Cast off.

With right side facing, rejoin yarn to rem sts and complete as first side.

LEFT FRONT

With 3¼mm (No 10/US 3) needles and B, cast on 43 sts. Beg with a k row, work 37 rows in st st.
Shape Neck
Cast off 5 sts at beg of next row. Dec one st at neck edge on foll right side row. Work 1 row. Mark side edge of last row. Dec one st at neck edge on next row and every foll alt row until 14 sts rem. Work 6 rows straight. Cast off.

RIGHT FRONT

Work as given for Left Front, reversing neck shaping.

SLEEVES

Join shoulder seams.
With 3¼mm (No 10/US 3) needles, B and right side facing, k up 60 sts between markers. Beg with a p row, work in st st, dec one st at each end of 2nd row and 5 foll 3rd rows. 48 sts. Work 4 rows. Beg with a p row (thus reversing fabric), work 5 rows in st st, inc one st at each end of 2nd row and foll alt row. 52 sts. Cast off.

COLLAR

With 3¼mm (No 10/US 3) needles and B, cast on 6 sts. Beg with a k row, work in st st, inc one st at beg of 3rd row and 8 foll 4th rows. 15 sts. Work 24 rows straight.
** **1st row** P4, yb, sl 1, yf, turn.
2nd row and 3 foll alt rows Sl 1, k to end.
3rd row P8, yb, sl 1, yf, turn.
5th row P12, yb, sl 1, yf, turn.
7th row As 3rd row.
9th row As 1st row.
10th row As 2nd row. **
Work 44 rows straight. Rep from ** to **. Work 24 rows straight. Dec one st at end of next row and 8 foll 4th rows. 6 sts.

Work 2 rows. Cast off.

POCKETS (MAKE 2)

With 3¼mm (No 10/US 3) needles and B, cast on 10 sts. Beg with a k row, work 10 rows in st st. P 1 row. K 1 row. Cast off.

BELT

With 3¼mm (No 10/US 3) needles and B, cast on 130 sts. K 1 row and p 1 row. Cast off.

TO MAKE UP

Join side and sleeve seams, reversing seams on cuffs. With crochet hook, B and beg below neck shaping, work 1 row of dc along straight edge of left front, along lower edge and up straight edge of right front to beg of neck shaping, working 3 dc into each corner. Do not turn. Join A and work 1 row of backwards dc (dc worked from left to right) along straight edge of right front to corner. Fasten off. Join A yarn at corner of left front and work 1 row of backwards dc along straight edge of left front. Fasten off. Rejoin B yarn at corner of left front and work 1 row of dc along lower edge. Fasten off. With crochet hook and B, work 1 round of dc along top edge of cuff, ss in first dc. Do not turn. Join A yarn and work 1 round of backwards dc. Fasten off. Sew on collar. With crochet hook, B and right side of collar facing, work 1 row of dc along outside edge. Do not turn. Join A and work 1 row of backwards dc. Fasten off. With crochet hook, attach B yarn to one front edge in line with neck shaping and work chain approximately 10cm/4in long for tie. Fasten off. Work tie in same way at opposit inside side seam. Work edging around belt in same way as on sleeves and along top edges of pockets as on collar. Sew pockets in place. With crochet hook and B, work loops at side edges for belt.

Golfing Bear

See Page
13

MATERIALS
Bear 4 25g hanks of Rowan
Lightweight DK.
Small amount of Brown yarn for
embroidery.
Pair of 2¾mm (No 12/US 2) knitting
needles.
Stuffing.
Outfit 2 50g hanks of Rowan DK
Tweed (A).
2 25g hanks of Rowan Lightweight DK
in each of Beige (B) and Mid Brown
(C) and 1 hank in each of Cream (D),
Light Blue, Rust, Dark Blue and
Yellow .
1 50g ball of Rowan True 4 ply Botany
in Cream (E).
Small amount of DK yarn in Dark
Brown.
Pair each of 2¾mm (No 12/US 2),
3 mm (No 11/US 2), 3¼mm (No 10/US
3), 3¾mm (No 9/US 4) and 4 mm (No
8/US 6) knitting needles.
Small size crochet hook.
3 buttons.
Length of shirring elastic.
Small amount of stuffing.

MEASUREMENTS
Bear approximately 36cm/14in high.

TENSIONS
32 sts and 40 rows to 10cm/4in
square over st st using Lightweight
DK yarn and 2¾mm (No 12/US 2)
needles.
28 sts and 33 rows to 10cm/4in
square over coloured patt using
Lightweight DK yarn and 3¾mm (No
9/US 4) needles.
22 sts and 30 rows to 10cm/4in
square over st st using Tweed DK
yarn and 4 mm (No 8/US 6) needles.
28 sts and 36 rows to 10cm/4in
square over st st using 4 ply yarn and
3¼mm (No 10/US 3) needles.

ABBREVIATIONS
See page 5.

NOTES
Read charts from right to left on right
side (k) rows and from left to right on
wrong side (p) rows. When working
colour pattern, strand yarn not in use
loosely across wrong side to keep
fabric elastic.

BODY (MAKE 2)
* With 2¾mm (No 12/US 2) needles cast
on 7 sts. K 1 row. Cont in st st, inc one st
at each end of next 2 rows and 5 foll alt
rows. 21 sts. Work 1 row.* Break off yarn.
Rep from * to *. K 1 row across both set
of sts. 42 sts. Work 25 rows straight. Dec
one st at each end of next row, 2 foll 4th
rows and 3 foll alt rows, then on every
row until 20 sts rem. Work 1 row. Cast
off.

BACK HEAD
With 2¾mm (No 12/US 2) needles cast
on 7 sts. K 1 row. Cont in st st, inc one st
at each end of next 2 rows, then at end
of foll 5 rows. Work 1 row. Inc one st at
beg of next 2 rows. 18 sts. Break off
yarn.
With 2¾mm (No 12/US 2) needles cast
on 7 sts. K 1 row. Cont in st st, inc one st
at each end of next 2 rows, then at beg
of foll 5 rows. Work 1 row. Inc one st at
end of next 2 rows. 18 sts. P 1 row
across both set of sts. 36 sts. Work 22
rows straight.
Next row K2 tog, k16, turn.
Work on this set of sts only. Dec one st at
each end of 2 foll 3rd rows, then foll alt
row. Mark beg of last row. Dec one st at
end of next row, each end of foll row and
at end of next row. 7 sts. Work 1 row.
Cast off.
Rejoin yarn at inside edge to rem sts, k
to last 2 sts, k2 tog. Dec one st at each
end of 2 foll 3rd rows, then foll alt row.
Mark end of last row. Dec one st at beg
of next row, each end of foll row and at
beg of foll row. 7 sts. Work 1 row. Cast
off.

RIGHT SIDE HEAD
With 2¾mm (No 12/US 2) needles cast
on 10 sts. K 1 row. P 1 row inc one st at
beg. Cont in st st, inc one st at each end
of next row and at beg of foll 6 rows,
then at end of next row. Inc one st at
each end of next row. Inc one st at end
of next row and at same edge on foll 3
rows. 26 sts. Work 11 rows straight. Mark
end of last row. Cast off 2 sts at beg of
next row. Dec one st at end of next row
and at same edge on foll 6 rows. Dec
one st at each end of next row, then at
end of foll row. Dec one st at each end of
foll alt row. Work 1 row. Dec one st at
end of next 3 rows. 9 sts. Work 1 row.
Mark end of last row. Cast off.

Bear

LEGS (MAKE 2)
With 2¾mm (No 12/US 2) needles cast on 50
sts. Beg with a k row, work 10 rows in st st.
Next row K25, turn.
Work on this set of sts only. Dec one st at
beg of next row and 3 foll alt rows, then
at end of next row and at beg of foll row.
19 sts. Work 1 row. Break off yarn and
rejoin at inside edge to secend set of 25
sts, k to end. Dec one st at end of next
row and 3 foll alt rows, then at beg of
next row and at end of foll row. 19 sts.
Work 1 row. P 1 row across both set of
sts. 38 sts. Work 21 rows.
Next row P19, turn.
Work on this set of sts only. Dec one st at
each end of next row and 2 foll alt rows,
then on 2 foll rows. 9 sts. Work 1 row.
Cast off. Rejoin yarn to rem sts and
complete as first side.

SOLE (MAKE 2)
With 2¾mm (No 12/US 2) needles cast
on 5 sts. K 1 row. Cont in st st, inc one st

at each end of next 3 rows and foll alt
row, then on foll 4th row. 15 sts. Work 11
rows straight. Dec one st at each end of
next row, foll 4th row, and on foll alt row,
then at each end of next 2 rows. 5 sts.
Work 1 row. Cast off.

ARMS (MAKE 2)
* With 2¾mm (No 12/US 2) needles cast
on 8 sts. Beg with a k row, work 2 rows in
st st. Cont in st st, inc one st at each end
of next row and foll alt row. Work 1 row.*
Inc one st at beg of next row. Work 1
row. Inc one st at each end of foll row. 15
sts. Work 1 row. Break off yarn. Rep from
* to *. Inc one st at end of next row. Work
1 row. Inc one st at each end of foll row.
15 sts. Work 1 row. K 1 row across both
set of sts. 30 sts. Inc one st at each end
of 2nd row and 3 foll 6th rows. 38 sts.
Work 14 rows straight.
Next row P19, turn.
Work on this set of sts only. Dec one st at
each end of next row and 2 foll alt rows,
then on 2 foll rows. 9 sts. Work 1 row.
Cast off. Rejoin yarn to rem sts and
complete as first side.

LEFT SIDE HEAD

Work as given for Right Side Head, reversing shapings by reading p for k and k for p.

HEAD GUSSET

With 2¾mm (No 12/US 2) needles cast on 20 sts. Work 10 rows in st st. Dec one st at each end of next row and 3 foll 4th rows, then on 3 foll alt rows. Work 3 rows. Dec one st at each end of next 2 rows. Work 2 tog and fasten off.

EARS (MAKE 4)

With 2¾mm (No 12/US 2) needles cast on 13 sts. Work 5 rows in st st. Dec one st at each end of next row and 2 foll alt rows, then on foll 2 rows. 3 sts. Cast off.

TO MAKE UP

Join instep, top and back leg seams, leaving an opening. Sew in soles. Stuff and close opening. Join arm seams, leaving an opening. Stuff and close opening. Join centre seam on each body piece. Join body pieces together, leaving cast off edge open. Stuff and gather open edge, pull up and secure. Join sides of head from cast on edge to first marker. Sew in head gusset, placing point at centre front seam and cast on edge in line with second markers on sides of head. Join centre seams of back head, then sew to front head, matching markers and leaving cast on edge open. Stuff and gather open edge, pull up and secure. Sew head to body. Attach yarn about 1cm/½in below top of one arm, thread yarn through body at shoulder position, then attach other arm, pull yarn tightly and thread through body again in same place, then attach yarn to first arm again and fasten off. Attach legs at hip position in same way as arms. Join paired ear pieces together and sew them in place. With Brown, embroider face features.

Sweater

BACK

With 3¼mm (No 10/US 3) needles and B, cast on 50 sts. Work 4 rows in k1, p1 rib, inc one st at centre of last row. 51 sts.
Change to 3¾mm (No 9/US 4) needles. Beg with a k row, work in st st and patt from chart 1 for 44 rows.
Shape Neck
Next row Patt 19, cast off next 13 sts, patt to end.
Work on last set of sts only. Work 1 row. Cast off 3 sts at beg of next row. 16 sts. Cast off.
With wrong side facing, rejoin yarn to

Chart 1

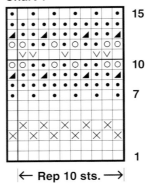

← Rep 10 sts. →

Chart 2

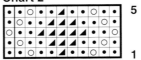

← Rep 10 sts. →

- • = Beige
- ◢ = Rust
- □ = Cream
- ◎ = Dark Blue
- ⊠ = Light Blue
- ⌵ = Yellow

rem sts, cast off 3 sts, patt to end. 16 sts. Work 1 row. Cast off.

FRONT

Work as given for Back until 30 rows of patt have been completed.
Shape Neck
Next row Patt 25, turn.
Work on this set of sts only. Dec one st at neck edge on next 4 rows, then on 5 foll alt rows. 16 sts. Work 2 rows. Cast off.
With right side facing, slip centre st onto a safety pin, rejoin yarn to rem sts and patt to end. Complete as first side.

NECKBAND

Join right shoulder seam.
With 3¾mm (No 9/US 4) needles, B and right side facing, k up 26 sts down left front neck, k st from safety pin, k up 26 sts up right front neck and 21 sts around back neck. 74 sts.
Next row P1, [k1, p1] 22 times, skpo, p1, k2 tog, [p1, k1] 12 times.
Rib a further 2 rows as set, dec one st at each side of centre front st. Cast off in rib, dec one st at each side of centre front st.

SLEEVES

Join left shoulder and neckband seam.

Mark side edges 32 rows down from shoulders on back and front
With 3¾mm (No 9/US 4) needles, D and right side facing, k up 61 sts between markers. Beg with a p row and 7th row of chart 1, work in st st and patt from chart for 10 rows.
Next row With D, p5, [p2 tog, p5] to end. 53 sts.
1st rib row With B, k1, [p1, k1] to end.
2nd rib row With B, p1, [k1, p1] to end.
Rep last 2 rows once more. With B, cast off in rib.

TO MAKE UP

Join side and sleeve seams.

Shirt

FRONT, BACK AND SLEEVES

Work as given for Front, Back and Sleeves of Shirt for Gardner Bear (see page 39), but using E instead of D.

COLLAR

With 3 mm (No 11/US 2) needles, E and right side facing, sl 3 sts from right front safety pin onto needle, k up 18 sts up right front neck, 18 sts around back neck and 18 sts down left front neck, then k3 sts from safety pin. 60 sts.
Next 2 rows Cast off 3, k to end. 54 sts.
Next row K2, k twice in next st, k to last 3 sts, k twice in next st, k2.
Rep last row 10 times more. K 1 row. Cast off loosely.

TIE

With 4 mm (No 8/US 6) needles and Dark Brown, cast on 90 sts. K 6 rows. Cast off.

TO MAKE UP

Join sleeve seams, then side seams to top of side edge borders. Sew on buttons.

Trousers

TO MAKE

With 2¾mm (No 12/US 2) needles and A, cast on 40 sts for one leg. Work 6 rows in k1, p1 rib.
Next row Rib 3, [inc in next st, rib 2] 12 times, rib 1. 52 sts.
Change to 4 mm (No 8/US 6) needles. Beg with a k row, work 20 rows in st st.
Shape Crotch
Cast off 5 sts at beg of next 2 rows. 42 sts. Work 20 rows straight. Now work 7 rows in k1, p1 rib. Cast off in rib.
Work one more. Join all seams. Thread 2 rows of shirring elastic on wrong side of rib at waist and fasten off securely.

Shoes

TO MAKE

With 2¾mm (No 12/US 2) needles and C, cast on 62 sts for upper part. Beg with a k row, work 8 rows in st st. Dec one st at each end of next 4 rows. 54 sts. Work 10 rows straight. K 3 rows. Cast off.

With 2¾mm (No 12/US 2) needles and C, cast on 24 sts for toe reinforcement. K 1 row.

1st row P20, yb, sl 1, yf, turn.
2nd row Sl 1, k16, yf, sl 1, yb, turn.
3rd row Sl1, p13, yb, sl 1, yf, turn.
4th row Sl 1, k10, yf, sl 1, yb, turn.
5th row Sl 1, p7, yb, sl 1, yf, turn.
6th row Sl 1, k4, yf, sl 1, yb, turn.
7th row As 5th row.
8th row As 4th row.
9th row As 3rd row.
10th row As 2nd row.
11th row Sl 1, p20.

K 1 row across all sts. Rep 1st to 11th rows again. K 1 row across all sts. Cast off.

With 2¾mm (No 12/US 2) needles and using two strands of C yarn together, cast on 4 sts for sole. Work in st st, inc one st at each end of 2nd row and 2 foll rows, then 2 foll alt rows and foll 4th row. 16 sts. Work 8 rows straight. Dec one st at each end of next row, foll 4th row and 2 foll alt rows, then at each end of next 2 rows. 4 sts. Work 1 row. Cast off.

With 2¾mm (No 12/US 2) needles and C, cast on 9 sts for fringe.

1st rib row K1, [p1, k1] to end.
2nd rib row P1, [k1, p1] to end.
Rep last 2 rows 3 times more.
Change to 4 mm (No 8/US 6) needles.
Next row Cast off 2, *sl st used in casting off back onto left hand needle, cast on 2 sts, cast off 4; rep from * until all sts are worked off.

Join front seam of upper part. Sew in sole. Fold toe reinforcement in half and join cast on and cast off edges together, stuffing widest part as you sew. Insert in shoe and secure in place. Place fringe over front seam and secure in position. With crochet hook and C, make chain approximately 13cm/5in long for bow. Tie bow and attach at centre of top of fringe. Make one more.

Sock Tops

TO MAKE

With 3¾mm (No 9/US 4) needles and B, cast on 50 sts.

Beg with a k row, work 6 rows in st st, inc one st at centre of last row. 51 sts. Work 5 rows in patt from chart 2. Cont in B only, p 1 row, dec one st at centre. 50 sts.

Change to 3¼mm (No 10/US 3) needles. Work 3 rows in k1, p1 rib. Cast off in rib. Make one more.

Cap

TO MAKE

With 3¾mm (No 9/US 4) needles and A, cast on 54 sts for brim. K 1 row.
Next row K4, [k twice in next st, k8] 5 times, k twice in next st, k4. 60 sts.
P 1 row.
Next row K19, [m1, k3] 8 times, k to end. Work 2 rows in st st.
Next row P20, [m1, p4] 8 times, p to end.
Work 2 rows.
Next row K20, [m1, k5] 8 times, k to end. 84 sts.
Next 2 rows P24, yb, sl 1, yf, turn, sl 1, k to end.
Next 2 rows P18, yb, sl 1, yf, turn, sl 1, k to end.
Next 2 rows P12, yb, sl 1, yf, turn, sl 1, k to end.
Next 2 rows P6, yb, sl 1, yf, turn, sl 1, k to end.
Work 1 row across all sts.
Next 2 rows K24, yf, sl 1, yb, turn, sl 1, p to end.
Next 2 rows K18, yf, sl 1, yb, turn, sl 1, p to end.
Next 2 rows K12, yf, sl 1, yb, turn, sl 1, p to end.
Next 2 rows K6, yf, sl 1, yb, turn, sl 1, p to end.
Cast off.

With 3¾mm (No 9/US 4) needles and A, cast on 8 sts for crown. Beg with a k row, work 2 rows in st st. Cont in st st, cast on 3 sts at beg of next 4 rows. Inc one st at each end of next 4 rows, 2 foll alt rows, then foll 4th row. 34 sts. Work 16 rows straight. Dec one st at each end of next row, 2 foll 4th rows, 3 foll alt rows, then on foll 6 rows. 10 sts. Cast off.

With 3¾mm (No 9/US 4) needles and A, cast on 24 sts for peak.
1st row K3, yf, sl 1, yb, turn.
2nd row and 3 foll alt rows Sl 1, p to end.
3rd row K5, yf, sl 1, yb, turn.
5th row K7, yf, sl 1, yb, turn.
7th row K9, yf, sl 1, yb, turn.
9th row K24.
10th row P3, yb, sl 1, yf, turn.
11th row and 3 foll alt rows Sl 1, k to end.
12th row P5, yb, sl 1, yf, turn.
14th row P7, yb, sl 1, yf, turn.
16th row P9, yb, sl 1, yf, turn.
18th row P22, yb, sl 1, yf, turn.
19th row Sl 1, k20, yf, sl 1, yb, turn.
20th row Sl 1, p19, yb, sl 1, yf, turn.
21st row Sl 1, k18, yf, sl 1, yb, turn.
22nd row Sl 1, p17, yb, sl 1, yf, turn.
23rd row Sl 1, k16, yf, sl 1, yb, turn.
24th row Sl 1, p15, yb, sl 1, yf, turn.
25th row Sl 1, k14, yf, sl 1, yb, turn.
26th row Sl 1, p12, yb, sl 1, yf, turn.
27th row Sl 1, k10, yf, sl 1, yb, turn.
28th row Sl 1, p8, yb, sl 1, yf, turn.
29th row Sl 1, k6, yf, sl 1, yb, turn.
30th row Sl 1, p to end.
31st row K24.
32nd row P15, yb, sl 1, yf, turn.
Work 29th to 19th rows in reverse order.
Next row Sl 1, p22.
Work 7th to 1st rows in reverse order.
Next row Sl 1, p3.
K 1 row across all sts. Work 16th to 10th rows in reverse order.
Next row Sl 1, k3.
Cast off.

Join back seam of brim. Placing centre of cast on edge to back seam, sew in crown. Fold peak in half and join row end edges together. Place cast on edge of brim inside open edge of peak and sew peak in position.

Small Tweed Bear in Jacket

See Page
14

MATERIALS

Bear 1 50g hank of Rowan DK Tweed. Small amount of Black yarn for embroidery.
Pair of 3¼mm (No 10/US 3) knitting needles.
Stuffing.
Jacket 1 100g hank of Rowan Recycled.
Pair of 6 mm (No 4/US 10) knitting needles.
2 buttons.

MEASUREMENTS

Bear approximately 23cm/9in high.

TENSIONS

24 sts and 32 rows to 10cm/4in square over st st using DK Tweed yarn and 3¼mm (No 10/US 3) needles.
15 sts and 30 rows to 10cm/4in square over garter st (every row k) using Recycled yarn and 6 mm (No 4/US 10) needles.

ABBREVIATIONS

See page 5.

Bear

LEGS (MAKE 2)

With 3¼mm (No 10/US 3) needles cast on 34 sts. Beg with a k row, work 10 rows in st st.
next row K10, cast off next 14 sts, k to end. 20 sts.
Work 19 rows across all sts. Cast off.

SOLES (MAKE 2)

With 3¼mm (No 10/US 3) needles cast on 14 sts. Work 10 rows in st st. Cast off.

BODY (MAKE 2)

With 3¼mm (No 10/US 3) needles cast on 28 sts. Work 30 rows in st st. Cast off.

ARMS (MAKE 2)

With 3¼mm (No 10/US 3) needles cast on 21 sts. Work 26 rows in st st. Cast off.

HEAD (MAKE 2)

Work as given for Arms.

EARS (MAKE 4)

Work as given for Soles.

TO MAKE UP

Join instep seam of legs. Rounding seam at top, join top and back leg seams, leaving an opening. Sew in soles tapering corners. Stuff and close opening. Make darts at centre of cast on and cast off edges of each body piece, making top darts longer. With right sides together, join body pieces, tapering corners and leaving top edge open. Turn to right side and stuff. Gather top edge, pull up and secure. Fold arms lengthwise and rounding seams at top and lower edges, join seams, leaving an opening. Stuff and close opening. With right sides of head pieces together and leaving cast on edge free, sew around edges, tapering corners at back edge and forming point at centre of front edge for nose. Turn to right side and stuff. Gather open edge, pull up and secure. Sew head in place. Attach yarn 1cm/¼in below top at centre of one arm, thread through body at shoulder position, attach other arm, then thread yarn through body in same place again, pull up tightly, attach yarn to first arm again and fasten off. Attach leg at hip position in same way as arms. With right sides of paired ear pieces together, work seam around edge, tapering corners and leaving cast on edge free. Turn to right side and close opening. Make a "dimple" in centre of each ear. Sew them in place. With Black, embroider face features.

Jacket

TO MAKE

With 6 mm (No 4/US 10) needles cast on 20 sts for back. Work in garter st for 15 rows.
Shape Sleeves
Cast on 8 sts at beg of next 2 rows. 36 sts. K 15 rows.
Shape Neck
Next row K14, cast off next 8 sts, k to end.
Work 7 rows on last set of sts only for right front. Cast on 5 sts at beg of next row. K 2 rows.
Buttonhole row K to last 4 sts, k2 tog, yf, k2.
K 5 rows. Cast off 8 sts at beg of next row. 11 sts. K 5 rows. Rep buttonhole row. K 10 rows. Cast off.
Rejoin yarn at inside edge to rem sts for left front. K 6 rows. Cast on 5 sts at beg of next row. K 10 rows. Cast off 8 sts at beg of next row. 11 sts. K15 rows. Cast off.
Join side and sleeve seams, reversing seam on last 3 sts of sleeves for cuffs. Turn back cuffs. Sew on buttons.

Tweed Bear in Duffel Coat

See Page
15

MATERIALS
Bear 6 50g hanks of Rowan DK Tweed (A).
Small amount of DK yarn in Black (B).
Pair of 3¼mm (No 10/US 3) knitting needles.
Stuffing.
Jacket 2 100g hanks of Rowan Recycled (C).
Pair of 6 mm (No 4/US 10) knitting needles.
3 buttons.

MEASUREMENTS
Bear approximately 43cm/17in high.

TENSION
24 sts and 32 rows to 10cm/4in square over st st using DK Tweed yarn and 3¼mm (No 10/US 3) needles.
14 sts and 25 rows to 10cm/4in square over moss st using Recycled yarn and 6mm (No 4/US 10) needles.

ABBREVIATIONS
See page 5.

Bear

RIGHT LEG
With 3¼mm (No 10/US 3) needles and A, cast on 24 sts. P 1 row.
Next row K1, [m1, k2] to last st, m1, k1.
P 1 row.
Next row K9, [m1, k1] 3 times, [k1, m1] 3 times, k12, [m1, k1] 3 times, [k1, m1] 3 times, k3.
P 1 row.
Next row K12, [m1, k2] 4 times, k16, [m1, k2] 4 times, k4. 56 sts.
Work 13 rows in st st.
Next row K11, cast off next 12 sts, k to end.
Work across all sts.
Next row P30, p2 tog tbl, p2, p2 tog, p8.
Next row K7, k2 tog, k2, skpo, k16, skpo, k1, k2 tog, k8.
Next row P7, p2 tog, p1, p2 tog tbl, p26. 36 sts.
** Work 6 rows. Inc one st at each end of next row and 2 foll 4th rows. 42 sts. Work 13 rows.
Next row K8, k2 tog, k1, skpo, k16, k2 tog, k1, skpo, k8.
Work 3 rows.
Next row K7, k2 tog, k1, skpo, k14, k2 tog, k1, skpo, k7.
Work 1 row.
Next row K6, k2 tog, k1, skpo, k12, k2 tog, k1, skpo, k6.
Work 1 row.
Next row K5, k2 tog, k1, skpo, k10, k2 tog, k1, skpo, k5.
Work 1 row.
Next row K4, k2 tog, k1, skpo, k8, k2 tog, k1, skpo, k4.
Next row P3, p2 tog tbl, p1, p2 tog, p6, p2 tog tbl, p1, p2 tog, p3.
Next row K2, k2 tog, k1, skpo, k4, k2

tog, k1, skpo, k2. 14 sts.
Cast off.

LEFT LEG
With 3¼mm (No 10/US 3) needles and A, cast on 24 sts. P 1 row.
Next row K1, [m1, k2] to last st, m1, k1.
P 1 row.
Next row K3, [m1, k1] 3 times, [k1, m1] 3 times, k12, [m1, k1] 3 times, [k1, m1] 3 times, k9.
P 1 row.
Next row K6, [m1, k2] 4 times, k16, [m1, k2] 4 times, k10. 56 sts.
Work 13 rows in st st.
Next row K33, cast off next 12 sts, k to end.
Work across all sts.
Next row P8, p2 tog tbl, p2, p2 tog, p30.
Next row K8, skpo, k1, k2 tog, k16, k2 tog, k2, skpo, k7.
Next row P26, p2 tog, p1, p2 tog tbl, p7. 36 sts.
Complete as Right Leg from ** to end.

ARMS (MAKE 2)
With 3¼mm (No 10/US 3) needles and A, cast on 15 sts. P 1 row.
Next row K1, [m1, k2] to end. 22 sts.
Beg with a p row, work in st st, inc one st at each end of 4 foll alt rows, then on every foll 4th row until there are 40 sts.
Work 19 rows straight.
Next row K7, k2 tog, k2, skpo, k14, k2 tog, k2, skpo, k7.
Work 3 rows.
Next row K6, k2 tog, k2, skpo, k12, k2 tog, k2, skpo, k6.
Work 1 row.
Next row K5, k2 tog, k2, skpo, k10, k2 tog, k2, skpo, k5.
Work 1 row.
Next row K4, k2 tog, k2, skpo, k8, k2

tog, k2, skpo, k4.
Next row P3, p2 tog tbl, p2, p2 tog, p6, p2 tog tbl, p2, p2 tog, p3.
Next row K2, k2 tog, k2, skpo, k4, k2 tog, k2, skpo, k2. 16 sts.
Cast off.

BODY
Begin at neck edge.
With 3¼mm (No 10/US 3) needles and A, cast on 24 sts. P 1 row.
Next row K1, [m1, k2] to last st, m1, k1.
P 1 row.
Next row K2, [m1, k3] to last st, m1, k1.
48 sts.
Work 7 rows in st st.
Next row K10, m1, k1, m1, k2, m1, k1, m1, k9, m1, k2, m1, k9, m1, k1, m1, k2, m1, k1, m1, k10.
Work 5 rows.
Next row K11, [m1, k2] 4 times, k9, m1, k2, m1, k11, [m1, k2] 4 times, k9.
P 1 row.
Next row K12, m1, k3, m1, k2, m1, k3, m1, k28, m1, k3, m1, k2, m1, k3, m1, k12. 76 sts.
Work 5 rows.
Next row K17, m1, k2, m1, k38, m1, k2, m1, k17.
Work 5 rows.
Next row K18, m1, k2, m1, k40, m1, k2, m1, k18.
Work 5 rows.
Next row K19, m1, k2, m1, k42, m1, k2, m1, k19. 88 sts.
Work 19 rows.
Next row K18, k2 tog, k2, skpo, k40, k2 tog, k2, skpo, k18.
P 1 row.
Next row K17, k2 tog, k2, skpo, k38, k2 tog, k2, skpo, k17.
P 1 row.
Next row K16, k2 tog, k2, skpo, k36, k2 tog, k2, skpo, k16.
P 1 row.
Next row K10, k2 tog, k3, k2 tog, k2, skpo, k3, skpo, k24, k2 tog, k3, k2 tog, k2, skpo, k3, skpo, k10.
P 1 row.
Next row K9, [k2 tog, k2] twice, [skpo, k2] twice, k6, skpo, k2, k2 tog, k8, [k2 tog, k2] twice, [skpo, k2] twice, k7.
P 1 row.
Next row K8, [k2 tog, k1] twice, [k1, skpo] twice, k6, skpo, k2, k2 tog, k6, [k2 tog, k1] twice, [k1, skpo] twice, k8.
P 1 row.
Next row K1, [k2 tog, k2] 3 times, [skpo, k2] 3 times, [k2 tog, k2] 3 times, [skpo, k2] twice, skpo, k1.
P 1 row.

Next row [K2 tog, k1] to end. 24 sts. Cast off.

HEAD

Begin at neck edge,
With 3¼mm (No 10/US 3) needles and A, cast on 24 sts. Beg with a k row, work 4 rows in st st.
Next row K1, [m1, k2] to last st, m1, k1. Work 3 rows.
Next row K2, [m1, k3] to last st, m1, k1. Work 3 rows.
Next row Cast on 4, k7, [m1, k4] to last st, m1, k1.
Cast on 4 sts at beg of next 5 rows. 84 sts. Work 14 rows. Mark each end of last row. Cast off 9 sts at beg of next 2 rows. Dec one st at each end of next 5 rows, then on 3 foll alt rows. 50 sts. P 1 row.
Next row K18, [skpo, k2] twice, [k2 tog, k2] twice, k3, skpo, turn.
Next row Sl 1, p20, p2 tog, turn.
Next row Sl 1, k20, skpo, turn.
Rep last 2 rows 3 times more, then work 1st of the 2 rows again.
Next row Sl 1, k20, sl 1, k2 tog, psso, turn.
Next row Sl 1, p20, p3 tog, turn.
Next row Sl 1, k20, skpo, turn.
Next row Sl 1, p20, p2 tog, turn.
Rep last 2 rows 4 times more. Work on rem 22 sts for gusset. Dec one st at each end of 5th row and foll 4th row, then on 2 foll alt rows. P 1 row.
Next row K2 tog, k2, skpo, [k2, k2 tog] twice. 10 sts.
Work 7 rows. Dec one st at each end of every row until 2 sts rem. Work 2 tog and fasten off.

EARS (MAKE 4)

With 3¼mm (No 10/US 3) needles and A, cast on 20 sts. Work in st st, dec one st at each end of 7th row, foll 4th row, then on 2 foll alt rows. Dec one st at each end of next row. 10 sts. Cast off.

NOSE

With 3¼mm (No 10/US 3) needles and B, cast on 9 sts. Work in st st, dec one st at each end of 3rd row and 2 foll alt rows. Work 1 row. Work 3 tog and fasten off.

TO MAKE UP

Join instep, top and inner seams of legs, leaving cast on edge free. Stuff and join sole seams. Join top and underarm seams of arms, leaving an opening. Stuff and close opening. Fold sides of body to centre and join cast off edge together, then join back seam. Stuff and gather open edge, pull up and secure. Join underchin and snout seam of head from cast on edge to markers. Sew in gusset. Stuff and gather open edge, pull up and secure. Sew head to body.
Attach yarn approximately 1cm/½in below top of one arm, thread through body at shoulder position, then attach other arm, pull up yarn tightly and thread through body again in same place, then attach yarn to first arm again and fasten off. Attach legs at hip position in same way as arms. Join paired ear pieces together and sew them in place. Sew on nose. With Black, embroider mouth and eyes.

Coat

BACK

With 6 mm (No 4/US 10) needles and C, cast on 33 sts.
1st row K1, [p1, k1] to end.
This row forms moss st. Work in moss st, dec one st at each end of 8th row and 2 foll 6th rows. 27 sts. Work 9 rows straight.
Shape Armholes
Cast off 3 sts at beg of next 2 rows. 21 sts. Work 24 rows.
Shape Shoulders
Cast off 6 sts at beg of next 2 rows. Cast off rem 9 sts.

LEFT FRONT

With 6 mm (No 4/US 10) needles and C, cast on 21 sts.
1st row P1, [k1, p1] to end.
This row forms moss st. Work in moss st, dec one st at beg of 8th row and 2 foll 6th rows. 18 sts. Work 9 rows straight.
Shape Armhole
Cast off 3 sts at beg of next row. 15 sts. Work 12 rows.
Shape Neck
Cast off 4 sts at beg of next row. Dec one st at neck edge on next 5 rows. 6 sts. Work 7 rows. Cast off.

RIGHT FRONT

Work as given for Left Front reversing all shapings and making buttonholes on 9th row and 2 foll 16th rows as follows:
Buttonhole row Patt 2, p2 tog, yrn, patt to end.

SLEEVES

With 6 mm (No 4/US 10) needles and C, cast on 31 sts. Work 32 rows in moss st as given for Back. Cast off.

HOOD

With 6 mm (No 4/US 10) needles and C, cast on 51 sts. Work 50 rows in moss st as given for Back. Cast off.

POCKETS (MAKE 2)

With 6mm (No 4/US 10) needles and C, cast on 9 sts. Work 14 rows in moss st as given for Back. Cast off.

TO MAKE UP

Join shoulder seams. Sew on sleeves, placing centre of sleeves to shoulder seams and sewing last 4 rows of sleeve tops to cast off sts at armholes. Join side and sleeve seams, reversing seam on last 10 rows for cuffs. Turn back cuffs. Fold hood in half and join cast off edge together. Sew on hood, pockets and buttons.

Jogging Bear

See Page
16

MATERIALS
Bear 4 25g hanks of Rowan Lightweight DK in Brown (A). Small amount of same in Black (B). Pair of 2¾mm (No 12/US 2) knitting needles. Stuffing.
Jogging suit 4 50g balls of Rowan Cotton Glace in Navy (C). Small amount of same in White. Pair each of 2¾mm (No 12/US 2) and 3¼mm (No 10/US 3) knitting needles. Length of shirring elastic.

MEASUREMENTS
Bear approximately 32cm/12½in high.

TENSIONS
32 sts and 40 rows to 10cm/4in square over st st using Lightweight DK yarn and 2¾mm (No 12/US 2) needles.
25 sts and 34 rows to 10cm/4in square over st st using Cotton Glace yarn and 3¼mm (No 10/US 3) needles.

ABBREVIATIONS
See page 5.

NOTES
Read chart from right to left on right side (k) rows and from left to right on wrong side (p) rows. Use separate lengths of contrast colour for each letter and twist yarns together on wrong side at joins to avoid holes.

Bear

RIGHT LEG
With 2¾mm (No 12/US 2) needles and A, cast on 24 sts. P 1 row.
Next row K1, [m1, k2] to last st, m1, k1.
P 1 row.
Next row K9, [m1, k1] 3 times, [k1, m1] 3 times, k12, [m1, k1] 3 times, [k1, m1] 3 times, k3.
P 1 row.
Next row K12, [m1, k2] 4 times, k16, [m1, k2] 4 times, k4. 56 sts.
Work 13 rows in st st.
Next row K11, cast off next 12 sts, k to end.
Work across all sts.
Next row P30, p2 tog tbl, p2, p2 tog, p8.
Next row K7, k2 tog, k2, skpo, k16, skpo, k1, k2 tog, k8.
Next row P7, p2 tog, p1, p2 tog tbl, p26. 36 sts.
** Work 6 rows. Inc one st at each end of next row and 2 foll 4th rows. 42 sts. Work 13 rows.
Next row K8, k2 tog, k1, skpo, k16, k2 tog, k1, skpo, k8.
Work 3 rows.
Next row K7, k2 tog, k1, skpo, k14, k2 tog, k1, skpo, k7.
Work 1 row.
Next row K6, k2 tog, k1, skpo, k12, k2 tog, k1, skpo, k6.
Work 1 row.
Next row K5, k2 tog, k1, skpo, k10, k2 tog, k1, skpo, k5.
Work 1 row.
Next row K4, k2 tog, k1, skpo, k8, k2 tog, k1, skpo, k4.
Next row P3, p2 tog tbl, p1, p2 tog, p6, p2 tog tbl, p1, p2 tog, p3.
Next row K2, k2 tog, k1, skpo, k4, k2 tog, k1, skpo, k2. 14 sts.
Cast off.

LEFT LEG
With 2¾mm (No 12/US 2) needles and A, cast on 24 sts. P 1 row.
Next row K1, [m1, k2] to last st, m1, k1.
P 1 row.
Next row K3, [m1, k1] 3 times, [k1, m1] 3 times, k12, [m1, k1] 3 times, [k1, m1] 3 times, k9.
P 1 row.
Next row K6, [m1, k2] 4 times, k16, [m1, k2] 4 times, k10. 56 sts.
Work 13 rows in st st.
Next row K33, cast off next 12 sts, k to end.
Work across all sts.
Next row P8, p2 tog tbl, p2, p2 tog, p30.
Next row K8, skpo, k1, k2 tog, k16, k2 tog, k2, skpo, k7.
Next row P26, p2 tog, p1, p2 tog tbl, p7. 36 sts.
Complete as Right Leg from ** to end.

ARMS (MAKE 2)
With 2¾mm (No 12/US 2) needles and A, cast on 15 sts. P 1 row.
Next row K1, [m1, k2] to end. 22 sts.
Beg with a p row, work in st st, inc one st at each end of 4 foll alt rows, then on every foll 4th row until there are 40 sts. Work 19 rows straight.
Next row K7, k2 tog, k2, skpo, k14, k2 tog, k2, skpo, k7.
Work 3 rows.
Next row K6, k2 tog, k2, skpo, k12, k2 tog, k2, skpo, k6.
Work 1 row.
Next row K5, k2 tog, k2, skpo, k10, k2 tog, k2, skpo, k5.
Work 1 row.
Next row K4, k2 tog, k2, skpo, k8, k2 tog, k2, skpo, k4.
Next row P3, p2 tog tbl, p2, p2 tog, p6, p2 tog tbl, p2, p2 tog, p3.
Next row K2, k2 tog, k2, skpo, k4, k2 tog, k2, skpo, k2. 16 sts.
Cast off.

BODY
Begin at neck edge.
With 2¾mm (No 12/US 2) needles and A, cast on 24 sts. P 1 row.
Next row K1, [m1, k2] to last st, m1, k1.
P 1 row.
Next row K2, [m1, k3] to last st, m1, k1. 48 sts.
Work 7 rows in st st.
Next row K10, m1, k1, m1, k2, m1, k1, m1, k9, m1, k2, m1, k9, m1, k1, m1, k2, m1, k1, m1, k10.
Work 5 rows.
Next row K11, [m1, k2] 4 times, k9, m1, k2, m1, k11, [m1, k2] 4 times, k9.
P 1 row.
Next row K12, m1, k3, m1, k2, m1, k3, m1, k28, m1, k3, m1, k2, m1, k3, m1, k12. 76 sts.
Work 5 rows.
Next row K17, m1, k2, m1, k38, m1, k2, m1, k17.
Work 5 rows.
Next row K18, m1, k2, m1, k40, m1, k2, m1, k18.
Work 5 rows.
Next row K19, m1, k2, m1, k42, m1, k2, m1, k19. 88 sts.
Work 19 rows.
Next row K18, k2 tog, k2, skpo, k40, k2 tog, k2, skpo, k18.
P 1 row.
Next row K17, k2 tog, k2, skpo, k38, k2 tog, k2, skpo, k17.
P 1 row.
Next row K16, k2 tog, k2, skpo, k36, k2 tog, k2, skpo, k16.
P 1 row.
Next row K10, k2 tog, k3, k2 tog, k2, skpo, k3, skpo, k24, k2 tog, k3, k2 tog, k2, skpo, k3, skpo, k10.
P 1 row.
Next row K9, [k2 tog, k2] twice, [skpo, k2] twice, k6, skpo, k2, k2 tog, k8, [k2 tog, k2] twice, [skpo, k2] twice, k7.

P 1 row.
Next row K8, [k2 tog, k1] twice, [k1, skpo] twice, k6, skpo, k2, k2 tog, k6, [k2 tog, k1] twice, [k1, skpo] twice, k8.
P 1 row.
Next row K1, [k2 tog, k2] 3 times, [skpo, k2] 3 times, [k2 tog, k2] 3 times, [skpo, k2] twice, skpo, k1.
P 1 row.
Next row [K2 tog, k1] to end. 24 sts.
Cast off.

HEAD
Begin at neck edge.
With 2¾mm (No 12/US 2) needles and A, cast on 24 sts. Beg with a k row, work 4 rows in st st.
Next row K1, [m1, k2] to last st, m1, k1.
Work 3 rows.
Next row K2, [m1, k3] to last st, m1, k1.
Work 3 rows.
Next row Cast on 4, k7, [m1, k4] to last st, m1, k1.
Cast on 4 sts at beg of next 5 rows. 84 sts. Work 14 rows. Mark each end of last row. Cast off 9 sts at beg of next 2 rows. Dec one st at each end of next 5 rows, then on 3 foll alt rows. 50 sts. P 1 row.
Next row K18, [skpo, k2] twice, [k2 tog, k2] twice, k3, skpo, turn.
Next row Sl 1, p20, p2 tog, turn.
Next row Sl 1, k20, skpo, turn.
Rep last 2 rows 3 times more, then work 1st of the 2 rows again.
Next row Sl 1, k20, sl 1, k2 tog, psso, turn.
Next row Sl 1, p20, p3 tog, turn.
Next row Sl 1, k20, skpo, turn.
Next row Sl 1, p20, p2 tog, turn.

Rep last 2 rows 4 times more. Work on rem 22 sts for gusset. Dec one st at each end of 5th row and foll 4th row, then on 2 foll alt rows. P 1 row.
Next row K2 tog, k2, skpo, [k2, k2 tog] twice. 10 sts.
Work 7 rows. Dec one st at each end of every row until 2 sts rem. Work 2 tog and fasten off.

EARS (MAKE 4)
With 2¾mm (No 12/US 2) needles and A, cast on 20 sts. Work in st st, dec one st at each end of 7th row, foll 4th row, then on 2 foll alt rows. Dec one st at each end of next row. 10 sts. Cast off.

NOSE
With 2¾mm (No 12/US 2) needles and B, cast on 9 sts. Work in st st, dec one st at each end of 3rd row and 2 foll alt rows. Work 1 row. Work 3 tog and fasten off.

TO MAKE UP
Join instep, top and inner seams of legs, leaving cast on edge free. Stuff and join sole seams. Join top and underarm seams of arms, leaving an opening. Stuff and close opening. Fold sides of body to centre and join cast off edge together, then join back seam. Stuff and gather open edge, pull up and secure. Join underchin and snout seam of head from cast on edge to markers. Sew in gusset. Stuff and gather open edge, pull up and secure. Sew head to body.
Attach yarn approximately 1cm/⅜in below top of one arm, thread through

body at shoulder position, then attach other arm, pull up yarn tightly and thread through body again in same place, then attach yarn to first arm again and fasten off. Attach legs at hip position in same way as arms. Join paired ear pieces together and sew them in place. Sew on nose. With Black, embroider mouth and eyes.

Top

BACK
With 2¾mm (No 12/US 2) needles and C, cast on 56 sts. K 5 rows.
Change to 3¼mm (No 10/US 3) needles.
Next row K to end.
Next row K2, p52, k2.
Rep last 2 rows twice more.** Work 66 rows in st st across all sts.
Shape Shoulders
Cast off 16 sts at beg of next 2 rows.
Cast off rem 24 sts.

FRONT
Work as given for Back to **. Work 2 rows in st st across all sts.
Next row K12C, k across 1st row of chart, k12C.
Next row P12C, p across 2nd row of chart, p12C.
Work a further 24 rows as set. Cont in C only, work 3 rows.
Next row P25, k6, p25.
Next row K.
Rep last 2 rows once more, then work 1st of the 2 rows again.
Next row K28, turn.
Work on this set of sts only.
Next row K3, p25.
Next row K.
Rep last 2 rows 5 times more.
Shape Neck
Cast off 6 sts at beg of next row. Dec one st at neck edge on foll 6 right side rows. 16 sts. Work 5 rows straight. Cast off.
With right side facing, join yarn to rem sts and k to end.
Next row P25, k3.
Next row K.
Complete to match first side.

SLEEVES
With 2¾mm (No 12/US 2) needles and C, cast on 44 sts. K 7 rows.
Change to 3¼mm (No 10/US 3) needles.
Beg with a k row, work in st st, inc one st at each end of 4 foll 3rd rows. 52 sts.
Work 4 rows straight. Cast off.

HOOD
With 3¼mm (No 10/US 3) needles and C, cast on 58 sts.
Next row K to end.

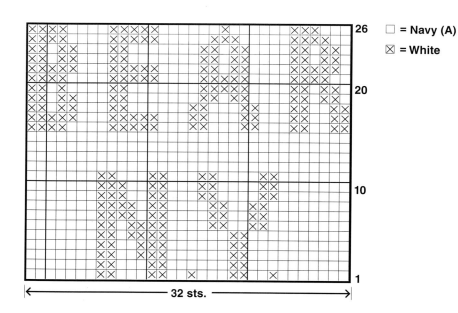

26
20
10
1

← **32 sts.** →

☐ = Navy (A)
☒ = White

Next row K3, p52, k3.
Rep last 2 rows 25 times more. Cast off.

TO MAKE UP

Join shoulder seams. Sew on sleeves, placing centre of sleeves to shoulder seams. Join sleeve seams and side seams to top of garter st borders. Fold hood in half and join cast off edge together. Sew on hood.

Trousers

TO MAKE

With 2¾mm (No 12/US 2) needles and C, cast on 56 sts.
Work 6 rows in k1, p1 rib.
Change to 3¼mm (No 10/US 3) needles.
Beg with a k row, work 16 rows in st st.
Shape Crotch

Cast off 3 sts at beg of next 2 rows. 50 sts. Work 30 rows straight.
Change to 2¾mm (No 12/US 2) needles.
Work 6 rows in k1 p1 rib. Cast off in rib.
Make one more.
Join all seams. Thread shirring elastic along wrong side of top rib and fasten off.

Edwardian Bear in Swimsuit

See Page
17

MATERIALS

Bear 4 25g hanks of Rowan Lightweight DK in Brown (A).
Small amount of same in Black (B).
Pair of 2¾mm (No 12/US 2) knitting needles.
Stuffing.
Swimsuit 1 25g hank of Rowan Lightweight DK in each of Navy (C) and Cream (D).
Pair of 3¼mm (No 10/US 3) knitting needles.
3 buttons.

MEASUREMENTS

Bear approximately 32cm/12½in high.

TENSIONS

32 sts and 40 rows to 10cm/4in square over st st on 2¾mm (No 12/US 2) needles.
28 sts and 36 rows to 10cm/4in square over st st on 3¼mm (No 10/US 3) needles.

ABBREVIATIONS

See page 5

Bear

RIGHT LEG

With 2¾mm (No 12/US 2) needles and A, cast on 24 sts. P 1 row.
Next row K1, [m1, k2] to last st, m1, k1. P 1 row.
Next row K9, [m1, k1] 3 times, [k1, m1] 3 times, k12, [m1, k1] 3 times, [k1, m1] 3 times, k3.
P 1 row.
Next row K12, [m1, k2] 4 times, k16, [m1, k2] 4 times, k4. 56 sts.
Work 13 rows in st st.
Next row K11, cast off next 12 sts, k to end.
Work across all sts.
Next row P30, p2 tog tbl, p2, p2 tog, p8.
Next row K7, k2 tog, k2, skpo, k16, skpo, k1, k2 tog, k8.
Next row P7, p2 tog, p1, p2 tog tbl, p26. 36 sts.
** Work 6 rows. Inc one st at each end of next row and 2 foll 4th rows. 42 sts. Work 13 rows.
Next row K8, k2 tog, k1, skpo, k16, k2 tog, k1, skpo, k8.

Work 3 rows.
Next row K7, k2 tog, k1, skpo, k14, k2 tog, k1, skpo, k7.
Work 1 row.
Next row K6, k2 tog, k1, skpo, k12, k2 tog, k1, skpo, k6.
Work 1 row.
Next row K5, k2 tog, k1, skpo, k10, k2 tog, k1, skpo, k5.
Work 1 row.
Next row K4, k2 tog, k1, skpo, k8, k2 tog, k1, skpo, k4.
Next row P3, p2 tog tbl, p1, p2 tog, p6, p2 tog tbl, p1, p2 tog, p3.
Next row K2, k2 tog, k1, skpo, k4, k2 tog, k1, skpo, k2. 14 sts.
Cast off.

LEFT LEG

With 2¾mm (No 12/US 2) needles and A, cast on 24 sts. P 1 row.
Next row K1, [m1, k2] to last st, m1, k1. P 1 row.
Next row K3, [m1, k1] 3 times, [k1, m1] 3 times, k12, [m1, k1] 3 times, [k1, m1] 3 times, k9.
P 1 row.

Next row K6, [m1, k2] 4 times, k16, [m1, k2] 4 times, k10. 56 sts.
Work 13 rows in st st.
Next row K33, cast off next 12 sts, k to end.
Work across all sts.
Next row P8, p2 tog tbl, p2, p2 tog, p30.
Next row K8, skpo, k1, k2 tog, k16, k2 tog, k2, skpo, k7.
Next row P26, p2 tog, p1, p2 tog tbl, p7. 36 sts.
Complete as Right Leg from ** to end.

ARMS (MAKE 2)

With 2¾mm (No 12/US 2) needles and A, cast on 15 sts. P 1 row.
Next row K1, [m1, k2] to end. 22 sts.
Beg with a p row, work in st st, inc one st at each end of 4 foll alt rows, then on every foll 4th row until there are 40 sts.
Work 19 rows straight.
Next row K7, k2 tog, k2, skpo, k14, k2 tog, k2, skpo, k7.
Work 3 rows.
Next row K6, k2 tog, k2, skpo, k12, k2 tog, k2, skpo, k6.
Work 1 row.
Next row K5, k2 tog, k2, skpo, k10, k2 tog, k2, skpo, k5.
Work 1 row.
Next row K4, k2 tog, k2, skpo, k8, k2 tog, k2, skpo, k4.
Next row P3, p2 tog tbl, p2, p2 tog, p6, p2 tog tbl, p2, p2 tog, p3.
Next row K2, k2 tog, k2, skpo, k4, k2 tog, k2, skpo, k2. 16 sts.
Cast off.

BODY

Begin at neck edge.
With 2¾mm (No 12/US 2) needles and A, cast on 24 sts. P 1 row.
Next row K1, [m1, k2] to last st, m1, k1. P 1 row.
Next row K2, [m1, k3] to last st, m1, k1. 48 sts.

Work 7 rows in st st.
Next row K10, m1, k1, m1, k2, m1, k1, m1, k9, m1, k2, m1, k9, m1, k1, m1, k2, m1, k1, m1, k10.
Work 5 rows.
Next row K11, [m1, k2] 4 times, k9, m1, k2, m1, k11, [m1, k2] 4 times, k9.
P 1 row.
Next row K12, m1, k3, m1, k2, m1, k3, m1, k28, m1, k3, m1, k2, m1, k3, m1, k12. 76 sts.
Work 5 rows.
Next row K17, m1, k2, m1, k38, m1, k2, m1, k17.
Work 5 rows.
Next row K18, m1, k2, m1, k40, m1, k2, m1, k18.
Work 5 rows.
Next row K19, m1, k2, m1, k42, m1, k2, m1, k19. 88 sts.
Work 19 rows.
Next row K18, k2 tog, k2, skpo, k40, k2 tog, k2, skpo, k18.
P 1 row.
Next row K17, k2 tog, k2, skpo, k38, k2 tog, k2, skpo, k17.
P 1 row.
Next row K16, k2 tog, k2, skpo, k36, k2 tog, k2, skpo, k16.
P 1 row.
Next row K10, k2 tog, k3, k2 tog, k2, skpo, k3, skpo, k24, k2 tog, k3, k2 tog, k2, skpo, k3, skpo, k10.
P 1 row.
Next row K9, [k2 tog, k2] twice, [skpo, k2] twice, k6, skpo, k2, k2 tog, k8, [k2 tog, k2] twice, [skpo, k2] twice, k7.
P 1 row.
Next row K8, [k2 tog, k1] twice, [k1, skpo] twice, k6, skpo, k2, k2 tog, k6, [k2 tog, k1] twice, [k1, skpo] twice, k8.
P 1 row.
Next row K1, [k2 tog, k2] 3 times, [skpo, k2] 3 times, [k2 tog, k2] 3 times, [skpo, k2] twice, skpo, k1.
P 1 row.
Next row [K2 tog, k1] to end. 24 sts.
Cast off.

HEAD
Begin at neck edge.
With 2¾mm (No 12/US 2) needles and A, cast on 24 sts. Beg with a k row, work 4 rows in st st.
Next row K1, [m1, k2] to last st, m1, k1.
Work 3 rows.
Next row K2, [m1, k3] to last st, m1, k1.
Work 3 rows.
Next row Cast on 4, k7, [m1, k4] to last st, m1, k1.
Cast on 4 sts at beg of next 5 rows. 84 sts. Work 14 rows. Mark each end of last row. Cast off 9 sts at beg of next 2 rows. Dec one st at each end of next 5 rows, then on 3 foll alt rows. 50 sts. P 1 row.
Next row K18, [skpo, k2] twice, [k2 tog,

k2] twice, k3, skpo, turn.
Next row Sl 1, p20, p2 tog, turn.
Next row Sl 1, k20, skpo, turn.
Rep last 2 rows 3 times more, then work 1st of the 2 rows again.
Next row Sl 1, k20, sl 1, k2 tog, psso, turn.
Next row Sl 1, p20, p3 tog, turn.
Next row Sl 1, k20, skpo, turn.
Next row Sl 1, p20, p2 tog, turn.
Rep last 2 rows 4 times more. Work on rem 22 sts for gusset. Dec one st at each end of 5th row and foll 4th row, then on 2 foll alt rows. P 1 row.
Next row K2 tog, k2, skpo, [k2, k2 tog] twice. 10 sts.
Work 7 rows. Dec one st at each end of every row until 2 sts rem. Work 2 tog and fasten off.

EARS (MAKE 4)
With 2¾mm (No 12/US 2) needles and A, cast on 20 sts. Work in st st, dec one st at each end of 7th row, foll 4th row, then on 2 foll alt rows. Dec one st at each end of next row. 10 sts. Cast off.

NOSE
With 2¾mm (No 12/US 2) needles and B, cast on 9 sts. Work in st st, dec one st at each end of 3rd row and 2 foll alt rows. Work 1 row. Work 3 tog and fasten off.

TO MAKE UP
Join instep, top and inner seams of legs, leaving cast on edge free. Stuff and join sole seams. Join top and underarm seams of arms, leaving an opening. Stuff and close opening. Fold sides of body to centre and join cast off edge together, then join back seam. Stuff and gather open edge, pull up and secure. Join underchin and snout seam of head from cast on edge to markers. Sew in gusset. Stuff and gather open edge, pull up and secure. Sew head to body.
Attach yarn approximately 1cm/½in below top of one arm, thread through body at shoulder position, then attach other arm, pull up yarn tightly and thread through body again in same place, then attach yarn to first arm again and fasten off. Attach legs at hip position in same way as arms. Join paired ear pieces together and sew them in place. Sew on nose. With Black, embroider mouth and eyes.

Swimsuit

FRONT
With 3¼mm (No 10/US 3) needles and C, cast on 22 sts for first leg. K 3 rows. Beg with a k row, cont in st st and stripe patt of 4 rows D and 4 rows C throughout, work 8 rows.* Break off yarn.
Work second leg as given for first leg to *.

Next row K to end, then k across first leg sts. 44 sts.**
Work a further 35 rows in stripe patt.
Divide for Opening
Next row K22, turn.
Work on this set of sts only.
Next row K3, p19.
Buttonhole row K19, k2 tog, yf, k1.
Keeping border of 3 sts at inside edge as set, work 7 rows. Rep last 8 rows once more, then work the buttonhole row again. Work 1 row.
Shape Neck
Next row K19 and turn; leave the 3 sts on a safety pin.
Dec one st at neck edge on next 3 rows, then on 4 foll alt rows. 12 sts. Work 3 rows straight. Break off yarn and rejoin at inside edge to second set of sts, k to end.
Next row P19, k3.
Next row K.
Rep last 2 rows 9 times more.
Shape Neck
Next row P19 and turn; leave the 3 sts on a safety pin.
Dec one st at neck edge on next 3 rows, then on 4 foll alt rows. 12 sts. Work 2 rows straight.
BACK
Next row P12, cast on 20 sts, p across first set of sts. 44 sts.
Work 68 rows.
Next row K22, turn.
Work 7 rows on this set of sts only for first leg. With C, k 3 rows. Cast off.
Rejoin yarn to rem sts and complete second leg to match first leg.

SLEEVES
Place markers 32 rows down from shoulder at side edges of back and front.
With 3¼mm (No 10/US 3) needles, C and right side facing, k up 54 sts between markers.
Beg with a p row, work 3 rows in st st. Cont in stripe patt as given for Front, dec one st at each end of 2nd row and every foll alt row until 36 sts rem. Work 2 rows. With C, k 3 rows. Cast off.

NECKBAND
With 3¼mm (No 10/US 3) needles, D and right side facing, sl 3 sts from right front safety pin onto needle, k up 12 sts up right front neck, 18 sts across back neck and 12 sts down left front neck, then k3 sts from left front safety pin. 48 sts. K 3 rows, dec one st at each end of first and 3rd row. Change to C and k 1 row. Cast off, dec first and last st.

TO MAKE UP
Join side, sleeve and inside leg seams. Sew on buttons.

Floral Bear

See Page

18

MATERIALS
2 50g balls of Rowan Cotton Glace in Navy (A).
Small amount of same in each of Green, Red and Pink.
Pair of 3 mm (No 11/US 2) knitting needles.
Stuffing.

MEASUREMENTS
Approximately 28cm/11in high.

TENSION
27 sts and 36 rows to 10cm/4in square over st st on 3 mm (No 11/US 2) needles.

LEGS (MAKE 2)
With 3 mm (No 11/US 2) needles and A, cast on 32 sts.
K 1 row.
Next row P3A, p8 sts of 1st row of chart, p10A, p8 sts of 1st row of chart, p3A.
Next row K3A, k8 sts of 2nd row of chart, k10A, k8 sts of 2nd row of chart, k3A.
Work a further 9 rows as set.
Next row With A, k12, cast off next 8 sts, k to end. 24 sts.
Next row P8A, p8 sts of 1st row of chart, p8A.
Next row K8A, k8 sts of 2nd row of chart, k8A.
Work a further 9 rows as set. With A, k 1 row.
Next row P1A, p8 sts of 1st row of chart, p6A, p8 sts of 1st row of chart, p1A.
Next row K1A, k8 sts of 2nd row of chart, k6A, k8 sts of 2nd row of chart, k1A.

ABBREVIATIONS
See page 5.

NOTES
Read chart from right to left on right side rows and from left to right on wrong side rows. When working in pattern, use separate lengths of contrast colours for each coloured area and twist yarns together on wrong side at joins to avoid holes. If preferred, knit pieces in A only and swiss darn (see diagram below) all flower motifs afterwards.

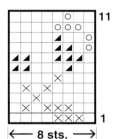

| | | | | | | | ○ | | 11 |

□ = Navy
☒ = Green
◢ = Red
◎ = Pink

← 8 sts. →

Work a further 9 rows as set. With A, k 1 row. Cast off.

SOLES (MAKE 2)
With 3 mm (No 11/US 2) needles and A, cast on 10 sts.
Beg with a k row, work 4 rows in st st.
Next row K1A, k8 sts of 1st row of chart, k1A.

Swiss Darning
Bring needle out to front at base of stitch to be covered. Insert needle under the base of stitch above then back at base. Emerge at base of next stitch to be covered

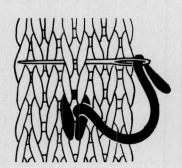

Next row P1A, p8 sts of 2nd row of chart, p1A.
Work a further 9 rows as set. With A, work 4 rows. Cast off.

BODY (MAKE 2)
With 3 mm (No 11/US 2) needles and A, cast on 24 sts. K 1 row.
**1st row P1A, p8 sts of 1st row of chart, p6A, p8 sts of 1st row of chart, p1A.
2nd row K1A, k8 sts of 2nd row of chart, k6A, k8 sts of 2nd row of chart, k1A.
3rd to 11th rows Rep last 2 rows 4 times more, then work 1st of the 2 rows again but working 3rd to 11th rows of chart.
12th row With A, k.
13th row P8A, p8 sts of 1st row of chart, p8A.
14th row K8A, k8 sts of 2nd row of chart, k8A.
15th to 24th rows As 3rd to 12th rows. **
Work 1st to 12th rows again. Cast off.

ARMS (MAKE 2)
With 3 mm (No 11/US 2) needles and A, cast on 21 sts.
Beg with a p row, work 3 rows in st st.
1st row K10A, k8 sts of 1st row of chart, k3A.
2nd row P3A, p8 sts of 2nd row of chart, p10A.
3rd to 11th rows Rep last 2 rows 4 times more, then work 1st of the 2 rows again, but working 3rd to 11th rows of chart.
12th row With A, p.
13th row K3A, k8 sts of 1st row of chart, k10A.
14th row P10A, p8 sts of 2nd row of chart, p3A.
15th to 24th rows As 3rd to 12th rows.
Work 1st to 11th rows again. With A, work 3 rows. Cast off.

HEAD (MAKE 2)
With 3 mm (No 11/US 2) needles and A, cast on 24 sts.
Beg with a k row, work 7 rows in st st.
Work as given for Body from ** to **. With A, work 2 rows. Cast off.

EARS
With 3 mm (No 11/US 2) needles and A, cast on 12 sts.
Next row K2A, k8 sts of 1st row of chart, k2A.
Next row P2A, p8 sts of 2nd row of chart, p2A.
Work a further 9 rows as set. Cast off.
Work one more piece in same way.
Using A only, make two more pieces in same way.

TO MAKE UP

Join instep seam on legs. Rounding seam at top, join top and back leg seams, leaving an opening. Sew in soles, rounding corners. Stuff and close opening. Make darts at centre of lower and top edges of body pieces, making top darts longer. With right sides together, join body pieces, tapering corners and leaving top edge open. Turn to right side and stuff firmly. Gather top edge, pull up and secure. Fold arms in half lengthwise and join seams, tapering corners and leaving an opening. Stuff firmly and close opening. Make darts at centre of lower edge of head pieces. With right sides of head pieces together and leaving cast on edge free, sew around pieces, tapering corners and forming point at centre front edge for nose. Turn to right side and stuff firmly. Gather open edge, pull up and secure. Sew head in place. Attach yarn 1cm/⅜in down from top at centre of one arm, thread through body at shoulder position, attach other arm, then thread yarn through body in same place again, pull up tightly, attach to first arm again and fasten off. Attach legs at hip position in same way as arms. With right side of paired ear pieces together, work seam around, tapering corners and leaving cast on edge free. Turn to right side and close opening. Sew them in place.

Floral and Gingham Bear

See Page 19

MATERIALS

2 50g balls of Rowan Cotton Glace in Cream (A).
1 ball of same in each of Dark Green (B), Light Green (C) and Red.
Pair of 3¼mm (No 10/US 3) knitting needles.
Stuffing.

MEASUREMENTS

Approximately 28cm/11in high.

TENSION

25 sts and 34 rows to 10cm/4in square over st st on 3¼mm (No 10/US 3) needles.

CHECK PATTERN

Rep of 4 sts, plus 2 edge sts.
1st row (right side) K2B, *2C, 2B; rep from *.
2nd row P2B, *2C, 2B; rep from *.
3rd row K2C, *2A, 2C; rep from *.
4th row P2C, *2A, 2C; rep from *.
These 4 rows form patt.

LEGS (MAKE 2)

With 3¼mm (No 10/US 3) needles and A, cast on 38 sts.
Next row (right side) K10 sts of 1st row of chart, k first row of check patt accross 18 sts, k10 sts of 1st row of chart.
Next row P10 sts of 2nd row of chart, p 2nd row of check patt across 18 sts, p10 sts of 2nd row of chart.
Work a further 7 rows as set.
Next row Patt 15, cast off next 8 sts, patt to end. 30 sts.
Next row K 1st row of check patt across 10 sts, k10 sts of 1st row of chart, k 1st row of check patt across 10 sts.
Next row P 2nd row of check patt across 10 sts, p10 sts of 2nd row of chart, p 2nd row of check patt across 10 sts.
Work a further 8 rows as set.
Next row K10 sts of 1st row of chart, k 1st row of check patt across 10 sts, k10 sts of 1st row of chart.
Next row P10 sts of 2nd row of chart, p 2nd row of check patt across 10 sts, p10 sts of 2nd row of chart.
Work a further 8 rows as set. With A, cast off.

ABBREVIATIONS

See page 5.

NOTES

Read chart from right to left on right side rows and from left to right on wrong side rows. When working in pattern, use separate lengths of contrast colours for each coloured area and twist yarns together on wrong side at joins to avoid holes. Strand yarn not in use loosely across wrong side over check part of pattern only. If preferred, swiss darn (see diagram page 57) all flower motifs afterwards.

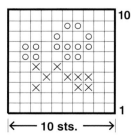

```
                                    10
          ○○
        ○        ○
    ○○  ○○○○
    ○○    ○○
      ✕  ✕
        ✕  ✕✕✕
        ✕      ✕✕
                                    1
```

|← 10 sts. →|

☐ **= Cream (A)**

☒ **= Light Green (C)**

⊙ **= Red**

SOLES (MAKE 2)

With 3¼mm (No 10/US 3) needles and B, cast on 14 sts.
Beg with a k row, work 18 rows in st st and check patt. With B, cast off.

BODY (MAKE 2)

With 3¼mm (No 10/US 3) needles and A, cast on 30 sts.
1st row (right side) K10 sts of 1st row of chart, k 1st row of check patt across 10 sts, k10 sts of 1st row of chart.
2nd row P10 sts of 2nd row of chart, p 2nd row of check patt across 10 sts, p10 sts of 2nd row of chart.
Work a further 8 rows as set.
11th row K 1st row of check patt across 10 sts, k10 sts of 1st row of chart, k 1st row of check patt across 10 sts.
12th row P 2nd row of check patt across 10 sts, p10 sts of 2nd row of chart, p 2nd row of check patt across 10 sts.
Work a further 8 rows as set. Rep last 20 rows once more. With A, cast off.

ARMS (MAKE 2)

Work as given for Body, but working 30 rows in patt .

HEAD (MAKE 2)

With 3¼mm (No 10/US 3) needles and A, cast on 30 sts.
1st row (right side) K10A, k 1st row of check patt across 10 sts, k10A.
2nd row P10A, p 2nd row of check patt across 10 sts, p10A.
Work a further 2 rows as set. Now work 1st to 20th rows as given for Body.
Next row K 3rd row of check patt across 10 sts, k10A, k 3rd row of check patt across 10 sts.
Next row P 4th row of check patt across 10 sts, p10A, p 4th row of check patt across 10 sts.
Work a further 2 rows as set. With A, cast off.

EARS (MAKE 4)

With 3¼mm (No 10/US 3) needles and B, cast on 14 sts.
Beg with a k row, work 10 rows in st st and check patt. With B, cast off.

TO MAKE UP

Join instep seam on legs. Rounding seam at top, join top and back leg seams, leaving an opening. Sew in soles, rounding corners. Stuff firmly and close opening. Make darts at centre of lower and top edges of body pieces. With right sides together, join body pieces, tapering corners and leaving top edge open. Turn to right side and stuff firmly. Gather top edge, pull up and secure. Fold arms in half lengthwise and join seams, tapering corners and leaving an opening. Stuff firmly and close opening. Make darts at centre of lower edge of head pieces. With right sides of head pieces together and leaving cast on edge free, sew around pieces, tapering corners and forming point at centre front edge for nose. Turn to right side and stuff firmly. Gather open edge, pull up and secure. Sew head in place. Attach yarn 1cm/⅜in down from top at centre of one arm, thread through body at shoulder position, attach other arm, then thread yarn through body in same place again, pull up tightly, attach to first arm again and fasten off. Attach legs at hip position in same way as arms. With right side of paired ear pieces together, work seam around, tapering corners and leaving cast on edge free. Turn to right side and close opening. Sew them in place.

Aviator Bear

See Pages
20/21

MATERIALS

Bear 4 25g hanks of Rowan Lightweight DK.
Small amount of Brown yarn for embroidery.
Pair of 2¾mm (No 12/US 2) knitting needles.
Stuffing.
Outfit 3 25g hanks of Rowan Lightweight DK in Dark Brown (A).
2 hanks of same in each of Beige (B) and Mid Brown (C).
1 hank of same in each of Cream (D), Black (E) and White (F).
Pair each of 2¾mm (No 12/US 2) and 3¼mm (No 10/US 3) knitting needles.
Cable needle.
Small size crochet hook.
Open ended zip fastener 10cm/4in long (see To make up of Jacket for adjustment of length).
Length of shirring elastic.
Small amount of stuffing.

MEASUREMENTS

Bear approximately 36cm/14in high.

TENSIONS

32 sts and 40 rows to 10cm/4in square over st st on 2¾mm (No 12/US 2) needles.
28 sts and 36 rows to 10cm/4in square over st st on 3¼mm (No 10/US 3) needles.

ABBREVIATIONS

See page 5.

Bear

LEGS (MAKE 2)

With 2¾mm (No 12/US 2) needles cast on 50 sts. Beg with a k row, work 10 rows in st st.
Next row K25, turn.
Work on this set of sts only. Dec one st at beg of next row and 3 foll alt rows, then at end of next row and at beg of foll row. 19 sts. Work 1 row. Break off yarn and rejoin at inside edge to second set of 25 sts, k to end. Dec one st at end of next row and 3 foll alt rows, then at beg of next row and at end of foll row. 19 sts. Work 1 row. P 1 row across both set of sts. 38 sts. Work 21 rows.
Next row P19, turn.
Work on this set of sts only. Dec one st at each end of next row and 2 foll alt rows, then on 2 foll rows. 9 sts. Work 1 row. Cast off. Rejoin yarn to rem sts and complete as first side.

SOLE (MAKE 2)

With 2¾mm (No 12/US 2) needles cast on 5 sts. K 1 row. Cont in st st, inc one st at each end of next 3 rows and foll alt row, then on foll 4th row. 15 sts. Work 11 rows straight. Dec one st at each end of next row, foll 4th row, and on foll alt row, then at each end of next 2 rows. 5 sts. Work 1 row. Cast off.

ARMS (MAKE 2)

* With 2¾mm (No 12/US 2) needles cast on 8 sts. Beg with a k row, work 2 rows in st st. Cont in st st, inc one st at each end of next row and foll alt row. Work 1 row.* Inc one st at beg of next row. Work 1 row. Inc one st at each end of foll row. 15 sts. Work 1 row. Break off yarn. Rep from * to *. Inc one st at end of next row. Work 1 row. Inc one st at each end of foll row. 15 sts. Work 1 row. K 1 row across both set of sts. 30 sts. Inc one st at each end of 2nd row and 3 foll 6th rows. 38 sts. Work 14 rows straight.
Next row P19, turn.
Work on this set of sts only. Dec one st at each end of next row and 2 foll alt rows, then on 2 foll rows. 9 sts. Work 1 row. Cast off. Rejoin yarn to rem sts and complete as first side.

BODY (MAKE 2)

* With 2¾mm (No 12/US 2) needles cast on 7 sts. K 1 row. Cont in st st, inc one st at each end of next 2 rows and 5 foll alt rows. 21 sts. Work 1 row.* Break off yarn. Rep from * to *. K 1 row across both set of sts. 42 sts. Work 25 rows straight. Dec one st at each end of next row, 2 foll 4th rows and 3 foll alt rows, then on every row until 20 sts rem. Work 1 row. Cast off.

BACK HEAD

With 2¾mm (No 12/US 2) needles cast on 7 sts. K 1 row. Cont in st st, inc one st at each end of next 2 rows, then at end of foll 5 rows. Work 1 row. Inc one st at beg of next 2 rows. 18 sts. Break off yarn.
With 2¾mm (No 12/US 2) needles cast on 7 sts. K 1 row. Cont in st st, inc one st at each end of next 2 rows, then at beg of foll 5 rows. Work 1 row. Inc one st at end of next 2 rows. 18 sts. P 1 row across both set of sts. 36 sts. Work 22 rows straight.
Next row K2 tog, k 16, turn.
Work on this set of sts only. Dec one st at each end of 2 foll 3rd rows, then foll alt row. Mark beg of last row. Dec one st at end of next row, each end of foll row

and at end of next row. 7 sts. Work 1 row. Cast off.
Rejoin yarn at inside edge to rem sts, k to last 2 sts, k2 tog. Dec one st at each end of 2 foll 3rd rows, then foll alt row. Mark end of last row. Dec one st at beg of next row, each end of foll row and at beg of foll row. 7 sts. Work 1 row. Cast off.

RIGHT SIDE HEAD
With 2¾mm (No 12/US 2) needles cast on 10 sts. K 1 row. P 1 row inc one st at beg. Cont in st st, inc one st at each end of next row and at beg of foll 6 rows, then at end of next row. Inc one st at each end of next row. Inc one st at end of next row and at same edge on foll 3 rows. 26 sts. Work 11 rows straight. Mark end of last row. Cast off 2 sts at beg of next row. Dec one st at end of next row and at same edge on foll 6 rows. Dec one st at each end of next row, then at end of foll row. Dec one st at each end of foll alt row. Work 1 row. Dec one st at end of next 3 rows. 9 sts. Work 1 row. Mark end of last row. Cast off.

LEFT SIDE HEAD
Work as given for Right Side Head, reversing shapings by reading p for k and k for p.

HEAD GUSSET
With 2¾mm (No 12/US 2) needles cast on 20 sts. Work 10 rows in st st. Dec one st at each end of next row and 3 foll 4th rows, then on 3 foll alt rows. Work 3 rows. Dec one st at each end of next 2 rows. Work 2 tog and fasten off.

EARS (MAKE 4)
With 2¾mm (No 12/US 2) needles cast on 13 sts. Work 5 rows in st st. Dec one st at each end of next row and 2 foll alt rows, then on foll 2 rows. 3 sts. Cast off.

TO MAKE UP
Join instep, top and back leg seams, leaving an opening. Sew in soles. Stuff and close opening. Join arm seams, leaving an opening. Stuff and close opening. Join centre seam on each body piece. Join body pieces together, leaving cast off edge open. Stuff and gather open edge, pull up and secure. Join sides of head from cast on edge to first marker. Sew in head gusset, placing point at centre front seam and cast on edge in line with second markers on sides of head. Join centre seams of back head, then sew to front head, matching markers and leaving cast on edge open. Stuff and gather open edge, pull up and secure. Sew head to body. Attach yarn about 1cm/¼in below top of one arm, thread yarn through body at shoulder position, then attach other arm, pull yarn tightly and thread through body again in same place, then attach yarn to first arm again and fasten off. Attach legs at hip position in same way as arms. Join paired ear pieces together and sew them in place. With Brown, embroider face features.

Jacket

BACK
With 3¼mm (No 10/US 3) needles and A, cast on 45 sts. Beg with a k row, work 14 rows in st st.
Shape Armholes
Cast off 3 sts at beg of next 2 rows. Dec one st at each end of next 4 rows. 31 sts. Work 20 rows straight.
Shape Neck
Next row K10, cast off next 11 sts, k to end.
Work on last set of sts only. Dec one st at neck edge on next 2 rows. 8 sts. Work 1 row. Cast off.
With wrong side facing, rejoin yarn to rem sts and complete as first side.

LEFT FRONT
With 3¼mm (No 10/US 3) needles and A, cast on 22 sts.
Next row (right side) K.
Next row K2, p20.
Keeping the 2 sts at front edge in garter st (every row k) and remainder in st st, work 12 rows more.
Shape Armhole
Cast off 3 sts at beg of next row. Work 1 row. Dec one st at armhole edge on next 4 rows. 15 sts. Work 13 rows straight.
Shape Neck
Cast off 3 sts at beg of next row. Dec one st at neck edge on next 4 rows. 8 sts. Work 6 rows straight. Cast off.

RIGHT FRONT
With 3¼mm (No 10/US 3) needles and A, cast on 22 sts.
Next row (right side) K.
Next row P20, k2.
Complete as given for Left Front, reversing shapings.

SLEEVES
With 3¼mm (No 10/US 3) needles and A, cast on 40 sts. Beg with a k row, work in st st, inc one st at each end of 5th row and 2 foll 6th rows. 46 sts. Work 5 rows straight.
Shape Top
Cast off 3 sts at beg of next 2 rows and 5 sts at beg of foll 6 rows. Cast off rem sts.

COLLAR
Join shoulder seams.
With 3¼mm (No 10/US 3) needles and D, cast on 3 sts.
1st row (right side) K3.
2nd row K winding yarn round needle three times for each st.
3rd row K dropping extra loops.
4th row Place cable needle in front of all loops of previous row, [pick up loop of corresponding st of first row and k tog with next st, thus enclosing cable needle] 3 times. Pull out cable needle when you need to use it again.
These 4 rows form patt. Cont in patt until collar fits around neck edge, ending with 4th row. Cast off.

WELT
Work as given for collar until welt fits along lower edge of fronts and back, ending with 4th row. Cast off.

CUFFS
Work as given for collar until cuff fits along lower edge of sleeve, ending with 4th row. Cast off.

TO MAKE UP
Join side and sleeve seams. Sew on welt and cuffs, then join cuff seams. Sew in sleeves. Buy the shortest length of open ended zip. Mark required length from lower edge and remove few "teeth" above markers. Bind over firmly at top to "stop" zip when done up, leaving 1cm/¼in above stoppers, cut off excess length. Sew in zip. Sew on collar.

Jodhpurs

TO MAKE
With 3¼mm (No 10/US 3) needles and B, cast on 50 sts for one leg. Beg with a k row, work 12 rows in st st.
Next row K24, k twice in next st, turn.
Work on this set of 26 sts only. Inc one st at inside edge on next 7 rows. 33 sts. Work 1 row. Break off yarn. Rejoin yarn at inside edge to rem 25 sts. Inc one st at inside edge on next 8 rows. 33 sts. Work 1 row. Work 3 rows across all sts. 66 sts.
Shape Crotch
Cast off 3 sts at beg of next 2 rows. Dec one st at each end of next 4 rows. 52 sts. Make 24 rows straight. Now work 5 rows in k1, p1 rib. Cast off in rib.
Make one more. Join all seams. Thread 2 rows of shirring elastic on wrong side of rib and fasten off securely.

Boots

TO MAKE
With 2¾mm (No 12/US 2) needles and C, cast on 62 sts for upper part. Beg with

a k row, work 8 rows in st st. Dec one st at each end of next 3 rows.

Next row K1, k2 tog tbl, p50, k2 tog, k1. 54 sts.

Next row K

Next row K2, p50, k2.

Rep last 2 rows 8 times more. K 3 rows. Cast off.

With 2¾mm (No 12/US 2) needles and C, cast on 24 sts for toe reinforcement. K 1 row.

1st row P20, yb, sl 1, yf, turn.

2nd row Sl 1, k16, yf, sl 1, yb, turn.

3rd row Sl 1, p13, yb, sl 1, yf, turn.

4th row Sl 1, k10, yf, sl 1, yb, turn.

5th row Sl 1, p7, yb, sl 1, yf, turn.

6th row Sl 1, k4, yf, sl 1, yb, turn.

7th row As 5th row.

8th row As 4th row.

9th row As 3rd row.

10th row As 2nd row.

11th row Sl 1, p20.

K 1 row across all sts. Rep 1st to 11th rows again. K 1 row across all sts. Cast off.

With 2¾mm (No 12/US 2) needles and using two strands of E yarn together, cast on 4 sts for sole. Work in st st, inc one st at each end of 2nd row and 2 foll rows, then 2 foll alt rows and foll 4th row. 16 sts. Work 8 rows straight. Dec one st at each end of next row, foll 4th row and 2 foll alt rows, then at each end of next 2 rows. 4 sts. Work 1 row. Cast off.

Join front seam of upper part to beg of garter st (every row k) border. Sew in sole. Fold toe reinforcement in half and join cast on and cast off edges together, stuffing widest part as you sew. Insert in boot and secure in place. With crochet hook and C, make chain approximately 41cm/16in long for lace. Lace boot. Make one more.

Hat

TO MAKE

With 3¼mm (No 10/US 3) needles and A, cast on 4 sts for left ear flap. K 20 rows. Cont in garter st (every row k), inc one st at each end of next row and 3 foll alt rows. 12 sts. K10 rows. Leave these sts on a holder. Work right ear flap as given for left ear flap, but leave sts on needle.

Next row Cast on 10, k to end, cast on 22, then k across sts of left ear flap, cast on 10. 66 sts.

K 1 row.

Next row [K3, m1] twice, k20, [m1, k5] 4 times, k14, [m1, k3] twice. 74 sts.

Beg with a k row, work 12 rows in st st.

Next row K7, [k2 tog, k1, skpo, k13] 3 times, k2 tog, k1, skpo, k8.

Work 3 rows straight.

Next row K6, [k2 tog, k1, skpo, k11] 3 times, k2 tog, k1, skpo, k7.

Work 3 rows straight.

Next row K5, [k2 tog, k1, skpo, k9] 3 times, k2 tog, k1, skpo, k6.

Cont in this way, dec 8 sts as set on 4 foll alt rows. 18 sts.

Work 1 row. Break off yarn, thread end through rem sts, pull up and secure. Join seam.

Scarf

TO MAKE

With 3¼mm (No 10/US 3) needles and F, cast on 12 sts. Work in garter st (every row k) until scarf measure 66cm/26in. Cast off.

Goggles

TO MAKE

With 3¼mm (No 10/US 3) needles and two strands of A yarn together, cast on 45 sts for back strap. K 4 rows. Cast off.

With 3¼mm (No 10/US 3) needles and two strands of A yarn together, cast on 65 sts for lens frame.

Next row Cast off 30, k4 sts more, turn.

K 3 rows on these 5 sts for bridge. Cast off.

Rejoin yarn to rem 30 sts. Cast off.

Join frame ends to bridge. Attach back strap.

English Gentleman Bear

See Page

22

MATERIALS

Bear 4 25g hanks of Rowan Lightweight DK.

Small amount of Brown yarn for embroidery.

Pair of 2¾mm (No 12/US 2) knitting needles.

Stuffing.

Outfit 2 50g balls of Rowan DK Tweed (A).

1 50g ball of Rowan True 4 ply Botany in each of Cream (B) and Yellow (C).

Small amount of 4 ply yarn in Red (D) and Brown (E).

Length of Gold lurex yarn.

Pair each of 3¼mm (No 10/US 3) and 4 mm (No 8/US 6) knitting needles.

Small size crochet hook.

5 buttons for jacket, 3 buttons for shirt, 2 buttons for waistcoat and 1 "watch" button for pocket watch.

Length of shirring elastic.

MEASUREMENTS

Bear approximately 36cm/14in high.

TENSIONS

32 sts and 40 rows to 10cm/4in square over st st using Lightweigh DK yarn and 2¾mm (No 12/US 2) needles.

22 sts and 30 rows to 10cm/4in square over st st using DK Tweed yarn and 4 mm (No 8/US 6) needles.

28 sts and 36 rows to 10cm/4in square over st st using 4 ply yarn and 3¼mm (No 10/US 3) needles.

ABBREVIATIONS

Ch = chain; **dc** =double crochet; **ss** = slip stitch.

Also see page 5.

Bear

LEGS (MAKE 2)

With 2¾mm (No 12/US 2) needles cast on 50 sts. Beg with a k row, work 10 rows in st st.

Next row K25, turn.

Work on this set of sts only. Dec one st at beg of next row and 3 foll alt rows, then at end of next row and at beg of foll row. 19 sts. Work 1 row. Break off yarn and rejoin at inside edge to secend set of 25 sts, k to end. Dec one st at end of next row and 3 foll alt rows, then at beg of

Next row and at end of foll row. 19 sts. Work 1 row. P 1 row across both set of sts. 38 sts. Work 21 rows.

Next row P19, turn.

Work on this set of sts only. Dec one st at each end of next row and 2 foll alt rows, then on 2 foll rows. 9 sts. Work 1 row. Cast off. Rejoin yarn to rem sts and complete as first side.

SOLE (MAKE 2)

With 2¾mm (No 12/US 2) needles cast on 5 sts. K 1 row. Cont in st st, inc one st at each end of next 3 rows and foll alt row, then on foll 4th row. 15 sts. Work 11 rows straight. Dec one st at each end of next row, foll 4th row, and on foll alt row, then at each end of next 2 rows. 5 sts. Work 1 row. Cast off.

ARMS (MAKE 2)

* With 2¾mm (No 12/US 2) needles cast on 8 sts. Beg with a k row, work 2 rows in st st. Cont in st st, inc one st at each end of next row and foll alt row. Work 1 row.* Inc one st at beg of next row. Work 1 row. Inc one st at each end of foll row. 15 sts. Work 1 row. Break off yarn. Rep from * to *. Inc one st at end of next row. Work 1 row. Inc one st at each end of foll row. 15 sts. Work 1 row. K 1 row across both set of sts. 30 sts. Inc one st at each end of 2nd row and 3 foll 6th rows. 38 sts. Work 14 rows straight.

Next row P19, turn.

Work on this set of sts only. Dec one st at each end of next row and 2 foll alt rows, then on 2 foll rows. 9 sts. Work 1 row. Cast off. Rejoin yarn to rem sts and complete as first side.

BODY (MAKE 2)

* With 2¾mm (No 12/US 2) needles cast on 7 sts. K 1 row. Cont in st st, inc one st at each end of next 2 rows and 5 foll alt rows. 21 sts. Work 1 row.* Break off yarn. Rep from * to *. K 1 row across both set of sts. 42 sts. Work 25 rows straight. Dec one st at each end of next row, 2 foll 4th rows and 3 foll alt rows, then on every row until 20 sts rem. Work 1 row. Cast off.

BACK HEAD

With 2¾mm (No 12/US 2) needles cast on 7 sts. K 1 row. Cont in st st, inc one st at each end of next 2 rows, then at end of foll 5 rows. Work 1 row. Inc one st at beg of next 2 rows. 18 sts. Break off yarn.

With 2¾mm (No 12/US 2) needles cast on 7 sts. K 1 row. Cont in st st, inc one st at each end of next 2 rows, then at beg of foll 5 rows. Work 1 row. Inc one st at end of next 2 rows. 18 sts. P 1 row across both set of sts. 36 sts. Work 22 rows straight.

Next row K2 tog, k16, turn.

Work on this set of sts only. Dec one st at each end of 2 foll 3rd rows, then foll alt row. Mark beg of last row. Dec one st at end of next row, each end of foll row and at end of next row. 7 sts. Work 1 row. Cast off.

Rejoin yarn at inside edge to rem sts, k to last 2 sts, k2 tog. Dec one st at each

end of 2 foll 3rd rows, then foll alt row. Mark end of last row. Dec one st at beg of next row, each end of foll row and at beg of foll row. 7 sts. Work 1 row. Cast off.

RIGHT SIDE HEAD

With 2¾mm (No 12/US 2) needles cast on 10 sts. K 1 row. P 1 row inc one st at beg. Cont in st st, inc one st at each end of next row and at beg of foll 6 rows, then at end of next row. Inc one st at each end of next row. Inc one st at end of next row and at same edge on foll 3 rows. 26 sts. Work 11 rows straight. Mark end of last row. Cast off 2 sts at beg of next row. Dec one st at end of next row and at same edge on foll 6 rows. Dec one st at each end of next row, then at end of foll row. Dec one st at each end of foll alt row. Work 1 row. Dec one st at end of next 3 rows. 9 sts. Work 1 row. Mark end of last row. Cast off.

LEFT SIDE HEAD

Work as given for Right Side Head, reversing shapings by reading p for k and k for p.

HEAD GUSSET

With 2¾mm (No 12/US 2) needles cast on 20 sts. Work 10 rows in st st. Dec one st at each end of next row and 3 foll 4th rows, then on 3 foll alt rows. Work 3 rows. Dec one st at each end of next 2 rows. Work 2 tog and fasten off.

EARS (MAKE 4)

With 2¾mm (No 12/US 2) needles cast on 13 sts. Work 5 rows in st st. Dec one st at each end of next row and 2 foll alt rows, then on foll 2 rows. 3 sts. Cast off.

TO MAKE UP

Join instep, top and back leg seams, leaving an opening. Sew in soles. Stuff and close opening. Join arm seams, leaving an opening. Stuff and close opening. Join centre seam on each body piece. Join body pieces together, leaving cast off edge open. Stuff and gather open edge, pull up and secure. Join sides of head from cast on edge to first marker. Sew in head gusset, placing point at centre front seam and cast on edge in line with second markers on sides of head. Join centre seams of back head, then sew to front head, matching markers and leaving cast on edge open. Stuff and gather open edge, pull up and secure. Sew head to body. Attach yarn about 1cm/½in below top of one arm, thread yarn through body at shoulder position, then attach other arm, pull yarn tightly and thread through body again in same place, then attach yarn to

first arm again and fasten off. Attach legs at hip position in same way as arms. Join paired ear pieces together and sew them in place. With Brown, embroider face features.

Jacket

BACK

With 4 mm (No 8/US 6) needles and A, cast on 21 sts for right side. K 1 row.

Next row (right side) K.

Next row K2, p19.

Rep last 2 rows 3 times more.

Next row K to last 2 sts, cast off last 2 sts.

Leave these 19 sts on a holder.

With 4 mm (No 8/US 6) needles and A, cast on 21 sts for left side. K 1 row.

Next row (right side) K.

Next row P19, k2.

Rep last 2 rows 3 times more. K 1 row.

Next row P to end, then p across sts on holder. 40 sts.

Work 8 rows in st st.

Shape Armholes

Cast off 3 sts at beg of next 2 rows. Dec one st at each end of next 2 rows. 30 sts. Work 20 rows straight.

Shape Neck

Next row K10, cast off next 10 sts, k to end.

Work on last set of sts only. Dec one st at neck edge on next 3 rows. 7 sts. Work 1 row. Cast off.

With wrong side facing, rejoin yarn to rem sts and complete as given for first side.

POCKET LININGS

With 4 mm (No 8/US 6) needles and A, cast on 8 sts for lower pocket. Beg with a k row, work 8 rows in st st. Leave these sts on a holder. Work one more.

With 4 mm (No 8/US 6) needles and A, cast on 5 sts for top pocket. Beg with a k row, work 6 rows in st st. Leave these sts on a holder.

LEFT FRONT

With 4mm (No 8/US 6) needles and A, cast on 24 sts. K 1 row.

1st row (right side) K.

2nd row K2, p22.

Rep last 2 rows once more.

Buttonhole row K20, k2 tog, yf, k2.

Work 2nd row then 1st row.

Next row K2, p7, k8, p7.

K 1 row.

Next row K2, p7, cast off knitwise next 8 sts, p to end.

Next row K7, k across st of lower pocket lining, k to end.

Keeping the 2 sts at front edge in garter st (every row k) and remainder in st st, work 1 row, rep the buttonhole row, then

work 5 rows.
Shape Armhole
Cast off 3 sts at beg of next row. Work 1 row. Rep the buttonhole row but dec one st at beg of row. Work 1 row, dec one st at end of row. 19 sts.
Shape Neck
Next row K to last 4 sts, turn; leave the 4 sts on a safety pin.
Next row P2 tog, p4, k5, p4.
K1 row.
Next row P2 tog, p3, cast off knitwise next 5 sts, p to end.
Next row K4, k across sts of top pocket lining, k4.
Dec one st at neck edge on next row and 5 foll alt rows. 7 sts. Work 9 rows straight. Cast off.

RIGHT FRONT
With 4 mm (No 8/US 6) needles and A, cast on 24 sts. K 1 row.
1st row (right side) K.
2nd row P22, k2.
Rep last 2 rows twice more. K 1 row.
Next row P7, k8, p7, k2.
K 1 row.
Next row P7, cast off knitwise next 8 sts, p to last 2 sts, k2.
Next row K9, k across sts of lower pocket lining, k to end.
Keeping the 2 sts at front edge in garter st and remainder in st st, work 8 rows.
Shape Armhole
Cast off 3 sts at beg of next row. Dec one st at armhole edge on next 2 rows. 19 sts.
Shape Neck
Next row K4 and sl these sts onto a safety pin, k to end.
Dec one st at neck edge on next row and 7 foll alt rows. 7 sts. Work 9 rows straight. Cast off.

SLEEVES
With 4 mm (No 8/US 6) needles and A, cast on 35 sts. K 2 rows, inc 4 sts evenly across last row. 39 sts. Beg with a p row, work in st st, inc one st at each end of 2nd row and 3 foll 4th rows. 47 sts. Work 3 rows straight.
Shape Top
Cast off 3 sts at beg of next 2 rows and 5 sts at beg of foll 6 rows. Cast off rem sts.

COLLAR
With 4 mm (No 8/US 6) needles and A, cast on 16 sts. Work in garter st, casting on 3 sts at beg of 2nd row and 7 foll rows. 40 sts. Work 5 rows straight. Cast off.

LAPELS
With 4 mm (No 8/US 6) needles, rejoin A yarn at inside edge of 4 sts on one front. Cont in garter st, inc one st at inside

edge on next row and 5 foll alt rows. 10 sts. Work 9 rows straight. Cast off. Work other front lapel in same way.

BELT
With 4 mm (No 8/US 6) needles and A, cast on 20 sts. K 4 rows. Cast off.

PATCHES (MAKE 2)
With 3¼mm (No 10/US 3) needles and E, cast on 4 sts. Cont in st st, inc one st at each end of 2nd row and foll row. 8 sts. Work 8 rows straight. Dec one st at each end of next 2 rows. 4 sts. Work 1 row. Cast off.

HANDKERCHIEF
With 3¼mm (No 10/US 3) needles and D, cast on 10 sts. K 2 rows.
Next row K1, p8, k1.
Next row K.
Rep last 2 rows 4 times more. Cast off knitwise.

TO MAKE UP
Join lapels to fronts, then join shoulder seams. Sew on collar, beginning and ending at centre of cast off edge of lapels. Join side and sleeve seams. Sew in sleeves. Catch down on wrong side pocket linings and the 2 cast off sts at centre of back. Sew on buttons. Place belt on back at desired position and secure in place with buttons. Sew on patches on sleeves. With B, embroider spots on handkerchief and place it in top pocket.

Trousers

TO MAKE
With 4 mm (No 8/US 6) needles and A, cast on 50 sts for one leg. Beg with a k row, work 2 rows in st st.
Next row K12, sl 1, k24, sl 1, k12.
Next row P.
Next row K5, k2 tog, k17, k2 tog, k24. 48 sts.
1st row (right side) K12, sl 1, k23, sl 1, k11.
2nd row P.
Rep last 2 rows 11 times more.
Shape Crotch
Cast off 3 sts at beg of next 2 rows. Dec one st at each end of next 4 rows. 34 sts. Work 25 rows straight. Cast off knitwise. Make one more leg.
With 3¼mm (No 10/US 3) needles and D, cast on 40 sts for brace. K 5 rows. Cast off. Make one more brace.
Join all seams, reversing seam on first 5 rows of legs for cuffs. Turn back cuffs. Sew on braces.

Shirt

BACK
With 3¼mm (No 10/US 3) needles and B, cast on 42 sts. Beg with a k row, work 22 rows in st st.
Shape Armholes
Dec one st at each end of next 4 rows. 34 sts. Work 17 rows straight.
Shape Neck
Next row P12, turn.
Work on this set of sts only. Dec one st at neck edge on next 3 rows. 9 sts. Work 1 row. Cast off.
With wrong side facing, sl centre 10 sts onto a holder, rejoin yarn to rem sts and p to end. Complete as given for first side.

LEFT FRONT
With 3¼mm (No 10/US 3) needles and B, cast on 23 sts.
1st row (right side) K.
2nd row K2, p to end.
Rep last 2 rows 4 times more.
Buttonhole row K to last 4 sts, k2 tog, yf, k2.
Keeping the 2 sts at front edge in garter st (every row k) and remainder in st st, work 11 rows.
Shape Armhole
Rep the buttonhole row, dec one st at beg of row. Dec one st at side edge on foll 3 rows. 19 sts. Work 8 rows straight. Rep the buttonhole row. Work 1 row.
Shape Neck
Next row K to last 4 sts, turn; leave the 4 sts on a safety pin.
Dec one st at neck edge on next 6 rows. 9 sts. Work 5 rows straight. Cast off.

RIGHT FRONT
With 3¼mm (No 10/US 3) needles and B, cast on 23 sts.
1st row (right side) K.
2nd row P to last 2 sts, k2.
Complete as given for Left Front, reversing shapings and omitting buttonholes.

SLEEVES
With 3¼mm (No 10/US 3) needles and B, cast on 36 sts. K 6 rows, inc 5 sts evenly across last row. 41 sts. Beg with a p row, work in st st, inc one st at each end of 4th row and foll 6th row. 45 sts. Work 11 rows straight.
Shape Top
Dec one st at each end of next 4 rows. 37 sts. Work 1 row. Cast off.

COLLAR
Join shoulder seams.
With 3¼mm (No 10/US 3) needles and right side facing, sl 4 sts from right front

safety pin onto needle, join A yarn and k up 13 sts up right front neck, 5 sts down right back neck, k centre back sts, k up 5 sts up left back neck and 13 sts down left front neck, k4 sts from safety pin. 54 sts.
Next row K.
Next row K2, p50, k2.
Rep last 2 rows 3 times more. K 3 rows. Cast off.

BOW TIE
With 3¼mm (No 10/US 3) needles and D, cast on 20 sts for main part. K 8 rows. Cast off.
With 3¼mm (No 10/US 3) needles and D, cast on 6 sts for tie. Cast off.

TO MAKE UP
Join side and sleeve seams. Sew in sleeves. Sew on buttons. Fold ends of main part of bow to centre and join them together. Place tie around centre and secure in position. Attach shirring elastic to bow.

Waistcoat

BACK
With 3¼mm (No 10/US 3) needles and C, cast on 46 sts. K 1 row. Beg with a k row, work 10 rows in st st.
Shape Armholes
Cast off 3 sts at beg of next 2 rows. Dec one st at each end of next 3 rows. 34 sts. Work 19 rows straight.
Shape Neck
Next row K12, turn.
Work on this set of sts only. Dec one st at neck edge on next 5 rows. 7 sts. Cast off.

With right side facing, sl centre 10 sts onto a holder, rejoin yarn to rem sts, k to end. Complete as given for first side.

POCKET LININGS (MAKE 2)
With 3¼mm (No 10/US 3) needles and C, cast on 9 sts. Beg with a k row, work 6 rows in st st. Leave these sts on a holder.

LEFT FRONT
With 3¼mm (No 10/US 3) needles and C, cast on 3 sts. K 1 row.
Next row P twice in first st, p to end.
Next row Cast on 3, k to last st, k twice in last st.
Rep last 2 rows twice more then work first of the 2 rows again.
Next row Cast on 4, k to last st, k twice in last st.
Next row P twice in first st, p to end. 25 sts.
K 1 row.
Next row P9, cast off knitwise next 9 sts, p to end.
Next row K7, k across sts of pocket lining, k to end.
Work 5 rows.
Shape Armhole and Neck
Next row Cast off 3, k to last 2 sts, k2 tog.
Work 1 row. Dec one st at each end of next row then at end of foll row and at each end of next row. 16 sts. Cont to dec at neck edge on on 5 foll alt rows then on 4 foll 3rd rows. 7 sts. Work 3 rows straight. Cast off.

RIGHT FRONT
Work as given for Left Front, but reading p for k and k for p and casting off purlwise sts on pocket top.

FRONT EDGING
Join shoulder seams.
With 3¼mm (No 10/US 3) needles, right side facing and C, k up 17 sts along lower edge of right front from side to point, 10 sts from point to front edge, 6 sts along straight edge, 25 sts along shaped edge to shoulder, 6 sts down right back neck, k centre back sts, k up 6 sts up left back neck, 25 sts along shaped edge of left front to beg of neck shaping, 6 sts along straight edge, 10 sts along lower edge to point and 17 sts from point to side. 138 sts. K 2 rows. Cast off.

ARM EDGINGS
With 3¼mm (No 10/US 3) needles, right side facing and C, k up 52 sts evenly around armhole edge. K 2 rows. Cast off.

POCKET WATCH
With crochet hook and C, make 6 ch, ss in first ch.
1st round Work 8 dc into ring, ss in first dc.
2nd round 1 dc in first dc, [2 dc in next dc, 1 dc in next dc] 3 times, 2 dc in last dc, ss in first dc. Break off C.
Join Gold and make chain approximately 6cm/2¼in long. Fasten off. Place loop of "watch" button through centre of ring and secure in position.

TO MAKE UP
Join side seams. Catch down pocket linings. Make 2 buttonholes on straight edge of left front by pushing large knitting needle through sts. Sew on buttons. Place watch in the pocket and attach end of chain to top button.

Fisherman Bear

See Page
23

MATERIALS
Bear 3 25g hanks of Rowan Lightweight DK.
Small amount of Brown yarn for embroidery.
Pair of 2¾mm (No 12/US 2) knitting needles.
Stuffing.
Outfit 1 50g ball of Rowan DK Handknit Cotton in each of Olive Green (A), Bright Green (B) and Light Green (C).
1 50g ball of Rowan Designer DK Wool in each of Beige (D) and Brown (E).
Pair each of 3¼mm (No 10/US 3) and

4 mm (No 8/US 6) knitting needles.
7cm/2¾in open ended zip fastener (see To make Up of Jacket for adjustment of length).

MEASUREMENTS
Bear approximately 27cm/10½in high.

TENSIONS
32 sts and 40 rows to 10cm/4in square over st st using Lightweight DK yarn and 2¾mm (No 12/US 2) needles.
20 sts and 28 rows to 10cm/4in square over st st using DK Handknit yarn and

4 mm (No 8/US 6) needles.
24 sts and 32 rows to 10cm/4in square over st st using Designer DK yarn and 4 mm (No 8/US 6) needles.

ABBREVIATIONS
See page 5.

NOTE
When working fish motifs, use separate lengths of yarn for each coloured area and twist yarns together on wrong side at joins to avoid holes.

Bear

LEGS (MAKE 2)

With 2¾mm (No 12/US 2) needles cast on 38 sts. Beg with a k row, work 8 rows in st st.

Next row K19, turn.

Work on this set of sts only. Dec one st at beg of next row and 2 foll alt rows, then at end of foll row. 15 sts. Work 2 rows. Break off yarn and rejoin at inside edge to second set of 19 sts, k to end. Dec one st at end of next row and 2 foll alt rows, then at beg of foll row. 15 sts. Work 2 rows. P 1 row across both set of sts. 30 sts. Work 14 rows.

Next row K15, turn.

Work on this set of sts only. Dec one st at each end of next 3 rows. 9 sts. Work 1 row. Cast off. Rejoin yarn to rem sts and complete as first side.

SOLE (MAKE 2)

With 2¾mm (No 12/US 2) needles cast on 4 sts. K 1 row. Cont in st st, inc one st at each end of next 2 rows and 2 foll alt rows. 12 sts. Work 9 rows straight. Dec one st at each end of next row and 2 foll alt rows, then on foll row. 4 sts. Work 1 row. Cast off.

ARMS (MAKE 2)

* With 2¾mm (No 12/US 2) needles cast on 7 sts. Beg with a k row, work 2 rows in st st. Cont in st st, inc one st at each end of next row and foll alt row. Work 1 row.* Inc one st at beg of next row. 12 sts. Work 1 row straight. Break off yarn. Rep from * to *. Inc one st at end of next row. 12 sts. Work 1 row. K 1 row across both set of sts. 24 sts. Inc one st at each end of 2nd row and 2 foll 6th rows. 30 sts. Work 11 rows straight.

Next row K15, turn.

Work on this set of sts only. Dec one st at each end of next 3 rows. 9 sts. Work 1 row. Cast off. Rejoin yarn to rem sts and complete as first side.

BODY (MAKE 2)

* With 2¾mm (No 12/US 2) needles cast on 5 sts. K 1 row. Cont in st st, inc one st at each end of next 2 rows and 3 foll alt rows. 15 sts. Work 1 row.* Break off yarn. Rep from * to *. K 1 row across both set of sts, inc one st at beg and end of this row. 32 sts. Work 19 rows straight. Dec one st at each end of next row and 2 foll 4th rows, then on 2 foll alt rows. 22 sts. Work 1 row. Cast off.

BACK HEAD

With 2¾mm (No 12/US 2) needles cast on 5 sts. K 1 row. Cont in st st, inc one st at each end of next 2 rows, then at beg of next 4 rows. Work 2 rows straight. Inc one st at beg of next 2 rows. 15 sts. Work 1 row. Break off yarn.

With 2¾mm (No 12/US 2) needles cast on 5 sts. K 1 row. Cont in st st, inc one st at each end of next 2 rows, then at end of foll 4 rows. Work 2 rows straight. Inc one st at end of next 2 rows. 15 sts. Work 1 row. K 1 row across both set of sts. 30 sts. Work 10 rows.

Next row P15, turn.

Work on this set of sts only. Dec one st at each end of next row and foll 4th row, then on foll alt row. Dec one st at beg of next row. Mark beg of last row. Dec one st at each end of next row and at beg of foll row. 5 sts. Work 1 row. Cast off. Rejoin yarn at inside edge to rem sts, p to end. Dec one st at each end of next row and foll 4th row, then on foll alt row. Dec one st at end of next row. Mark end of last row. Dec one st at each end of next row and at end of foll row. 5 sts. Work 1 row. Cast off.

RIGHT SIDE HEAD

With 2¾mm (No 12/US 2) needles cast on 8 sts. K 1 row. P 1 row inc one st at beg. Cont in st st, inc one st at each end of next row and at beg of foll 4 rows, then at end of next row and beg of foll row. Inc one st at each end of next row, then at beg of foll row and end of next row. 21 sts. Work 8 rows straight. Mark end of last row. Cast off 2 sts at beg of next row. Work 1 row. Dec one st at beg of next row and end of foll row. Dec one st at each end of next row, then at end of foll row, beg of next row and end of foll row. Dec one st at each end of next row and at end of foll row. Dec one st at each end of next row. 7 sts. Work 1 row. Mark beg of last row. Cast off.

LEFT SIDE HEAD

Work as given for Right Side Head, reversing shapings by reading p for k and k for p.

HEAD GUSSET

With 2¾mm (No 12/US 2) needles cast on 15 sts. Work 6 rows in st st. Dec one st at each end of next row and 3 foll 4th rows, then on foll alt row. Work 3 rows straight. Dec one st at each end of next row. Work 3 tog and fasten off.

EARS (MAKE 4)

With 2¾mm (No 12/US 2) needles cast on 9 sts. Work 4 rows in st st. Dec one st at each end of next row and foll alt row, then on foll row. 3 sts. Cast off.

TO MAKE UP

Join instep, top and back leg seams, leaving an opening. Sew in soles. Stuff and close opening. Join arm seams, leaving an opening. Stuff and close opening. Join centre seam of each body piece. Join body pieces together, leaving cast off edge open. Stuff and gather open edge, pull up and secure. Join sides of head from cast on edge to first marker. Sew in head gusset, placing point at centre front seam and cast on edge in line with second marker on sides of head. Join centre seams of back head, then sew to front head, matching markers and leaving cast on edge open. Stuff and gather open edge, pull up and secure. Sew head to body. Attach yarn approximately 1cm/¼in below top of one arm, thread yarn through body at shoulder position, then attach other arm, pull yarn tightly and thread through body again in same place, then attach yarn to first arm again and fasten off. Attach legs at hip position in same way as arms. Join paired ear pieces together and sew them in place. With Brown, embroider face features.

Trousers

TO MAKE

With 4 mm (No 8/US 6) needles and A, cast on 28 sts for leg. K 4 rows, inc 2 sts evenly across last row. 30 sts. Beg with a p row, work 13 rows in st st.

Shape Crotch

Cast off 3 sts at beg of next 2 rows. 24 sts. Work 17 rows straight. K 2 rows. Cast off. Make one more.

With 4 mm (No 8/US 6) needles and A, cast on 24 sts for strap. K 2 rows. Cast off. Make one more.

Join all seams. Sew on ends of straps, crossing straps over at back.

Jacket

BACK

With 3¼mm (No 10/US 3) needles and E, cast on 40 sts. Work 4 rows in k1, p1 rib. Change to 4 mm (No 8/US 6) needles and D.

Beg with a k row, work 5 rows in st st.

Next row P4D, reading chart from left to right p across 1st row of chart, p6D, reading chart from right to left p across 1st row of chart, p4D.

Next row K4D, reading chart from left to right k across 2nd row of chart, k6D, reading chart from right to left k across 2nd row of chart, k4D.

Work a further 13 rows as set. Cont in D only, work 10 rows. Cast off.

LEFT FRONT

With 3¼mm (No 10/US 3) needles and E, cast on 21 sts.

1st rib row [K1, p1] 9 times, k3.
2nd rib row K3, [k1, p1] to end.
Rep last 2 rows once more.
Change to 4 mm (No 8/US 6) needles.
Twisting yarns together on wrong side when changing colour, work as follows:
Next row K18D, 3E.
Next row K3E, p18D.
Work a further 3 rows as set.
Next row K3E, p2D, reading chart from right to left p across 1st row of chart, p3D.
Next row K3D, reading chart from left to right k across 2nd row, k2D, 3E.
Work a further 12 rows as set.
Shape Neck
Next row K3E and slip these 3 sts onto safety pin, patt to end.
Cont in D only, dec one st at neck edge on next 5 rows. 13 sts. Work 5 rows. Cast off.

RIGHT FRONT

With 3¼mm (No 10/US 3) needles and E, cast on 21 sts.

1st rib row K3, [p1, k1] to end.
2nd rib row [P1, k1] 9 times, k3.
Rep last 2 rows once more.
Change to 4 mm (No 8/US 6) needles.
Twisting yarns together on wrong side when changing colour, work as follows:
Next row K3E, 18D.
Next row P18D, k3E.
Work a further 3 rows as set.
Next row P3D, reading chart from left to right p across 1st row of chart, p2D, k3E.
Next row K3E, 2D, reading chart from right to left k across 2nd row of chart, k3D.
Complete to match Left Front.

SLEEVES

Join shoulder seams. Mark side edges 20 rows down from shoulders on back and fronts.
With 4 mm (No 8/US 6) needles, D and

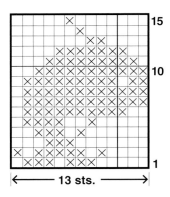

= Beige (D)

= Brown (E)

right side facing, k up 36 sts between markers. Beg with a p row, work 8 rows in st st. With E, p 1 row, dec 6 sts evenly. 30 sts.
Change to 3¼mm (No 10/US 3) needles. Work 4 rows in k1, p1 rib. Cast off in rib.

COLLAR

With 3¼mm (No 10/US 3) needles, rejoin E yarn at inside edge to the 3 sts on right front safety pin. Cont in garter st (every row k), inc one st at inside edge on next row and every foll alt row until there are 17 sts.
Change to 4 mm (No 8/US 6) needles. Cont in garter st until collar fits up right front to centre of back neck. Cast off. Work left side of collar in same way.

TO MAKE UP

Join side and sleeve seams. Join back seam of collar. Sew collar in position. Buy shortest length of open ended zip fastener. Mark required length from lower edge and remove few "teeth" above markers. Bind over firmly at top to "stop" when done up. Leaving 1cm/¼in above stoppers, cut off excess length. Sew in zip.

Waders

With 4 mm (No 8/US 6) needles and B, cast on 34 sts for upper part. Beg with a k row, work 6 rows in st st.
Next row K15, k2 tog, skpo, k15.
P 1 row.
Next row K14, k2 tog, skpo, k14.
P 1 row.
Next row K13, k2 tog, skpo, k13.
Next row P12, p2 tog tbl, p2 tog, p12. 26 sts.
Cont in st st, inc one st at each end of 3rd row and 2 foll 4th rows. 32 sts. Work 1 row. K 3 rows. Cast off.
With 4 mm (No 8/US 6) needles and B, cast on 8 sts for sole. Work in st st, inc one st at each end of 2 foll alt rows. Work 10 rows straight. Dec one st at each end of next row and foll alt row. Work 1 row. Cast off.
Join back seam of upper part, then sew in sole. Make one more.

Hat

TO MAKE

With 4 mm (No 8/US 6) needles and C, cast on 70 sts for brim. K 5 rows.
Next row K8, [k2 tog, k2] 14 times, k6. 56 sts.
P 1 row.
Next row K5, [k2 tog, k2] 12 times, k3. Work 10 rows in st st.
Next row P3, [p2 tog, p2] 10 times, p1. Cast off.
With 4 mm (No 8/US 6) needles and C, cast on 8 sts for crown. Work in st st, inc one st at each end of 2 foll alt rows. Work 8 rows straight. Dec one st at each end of next row and foll alt row. Work 1 row. Cast off.
Join back seam of brim, then sew in crown.

Small Star Bear

See Page
24

MATERIALS
Bear 2 25g hanks of Rowan Lightweight DK.
Small amount of Brown yarn for embroidery.
Pair of 2¾mm (No 12/US 2) knitting needles.
Stuffing.
Jumper 1 25g hank of Rowan Lightweight DK in Navy (A).
Small amount of same in Cream.
Pair of 3¼mm (No 10/US 3) knitting needles.

MEASUREMENTS
Bear approximately 18cm/7in high.

TENSIONS
32 sts and 40 rows to 10cm/4in square over st st on 2¾mm (No 12/US 2) needles.
28 sts and 36 rows to 10cm/4in square over st st on 3¼mm (No 10/US 3) needles.

ABBREVIATIONS
See page 00.

NOTES
Read chart from right to left on right side (k) rows and from left to right on wrong side (p) rows. When working star motif, use separate lengths of yarns for each coloured area and twist yarns together on wrong side at joins to avoid holes.

Bear

LEGS (MAKE 2)
With 2¾mm (No 12/US 2) needles cast on 26 sts. Beg with a k row, work 5 rows in st st.
Next row P13, turn.
Work on this first set of sts only. Dec one st at beg of next row and foll alt row, then at end of foll row. 10 sts. Break off yarn and rejoin at inside edge to second set of 13 sts, p to end. Dec one st at end of next row and foll alt row, then at beg of foll row. 10 sts. K 1 row across both sets of sts. 20 sts. Work 10 rows.
Next row P10, turn.
Work on this set of sts only. Dec one st at each end of next 2 rows. 6 sts. Work 1 row. Cast off. Rejoin yarn to rem sts and complete as first side.

SOLES (MAKE 2)
With 2¾mm (No 12/US 2) needles cast on 3 sts. K 1 row. Cont in st st, inc one st at each end of next 2 rows and foll alt row. 9 sts. Work 6 rows straight. Dec one st at each end of next row and foll alt row, then on foll row. 3 sts. P 1 row. Cast off.

ARMS (MAKE 2)
* With 2¾mm (No 12/US 2) needles cast on 4 sts. Beg with a k row, work in st st, inc one st at each end of 3rd row and foll alt row. 8 sts. P 1 row.* Break off yarn. Work from * to *. K 1 row across both sets of sts. 16 sts. Inc one st at each end of 2nd row and foll 4th row. 20 sts. Work 9 rows straight.

Next row K10, turn.
Work on this set of sts only. Dec one st at each end of next 2 rows. 6 sts. Work 1 row. Cast off. Rejoin yarn to rem sts and complete as first side.

BODY (MAKE 2)
* With 2¾mm (No 12/US 2) needles cast on 3 sts. K 1 row. Cont in st st, inc one st at each end of next 2 rows and 2 foll alt rows. 11 sts.* Break off yarn. Work from * to *. P 1 row across both sets of sts. 22 sts. Work 12 rows straight. Dec one st at each end of next row and 2 foll 3rd rows, then on foll alt row. 14 sts. P1 row. Cast off.

BACK HEAD
With 2¾mm (No 12/US 2) needles cast on 3 sts. K 1 row. Cont in st st, inc one st at each end of next 2 rows, then at end of 3 foll rows. Work 1 row. Inc one st at beg of next row. 11 sts. K1 row. Break off yarn.
With 2¾mm (No 12/US 2) needles cast on 3 sts. K 1 row. Cont in st st, inc one st at each end of next 2 rows, then at beg of 3 foll rows. Work 1 row. Inc one st at end of next row. 11 sts. K 1 row. P 1 row across both sets of sts. 22 sts. Work 6 rows straight.
Next row K11, turn.
Work on this set of sts only. Dec one st at each end of next row. Work 1 row. Dec one st at end of next 3 rows. Mark end of last row. Dec one st at each end of next row. 4 sts. Work 1 row. Cast off. Rejoin yarn at inside edge to rem sts and k to end. Dec one st at each end of next row. Work 1 row. Dec one st at beg

of next 3 rows. Mark beg of last row. Dec one st at each end of next row. 4 sts. Work 1 row. Cast off.

RIGHT SIDE HEAD
With 2¾mm (No 12/US 2) needles cast on 6 sts. K 1 row. P 1 row, inc one st at beg. Cont in st st, inc one st at each end of next row, then at beg of foll 4 rows. Inc one st at end of next row and at beg of foll row. 15 sts. Work 5 rows straight. Mark end of last row. Cast off 2 sts at beg of next row. Dec one st at end of next row and at beg of foll row. * Dec one st at each end of next row and at beg of foll row.* Rep from * to *. 5 sts. Work 1 row. Mark beg of last row. Cast off.

LEFT SIDE HEAD
Work as given for Right Side Head, reversing shapings by reading p for k and k for p.

HEAD GUSSET
With 2¾mm (No 12/US 2) needles cast on 11 sts. Beg with a k row, work 4 rows in st st. Dec one st at each end of next row and foll alt row, then on foll row. Work 2 rows. Dec one st at each end of next row. Work 1 row. K3 tog and fasten off.

EARS (MAKE 4)
With 2¾mm (No 12/US 2) needles cast on 6 sts. Work 3 rows in st st. Dec one st at each end of next 2 rows. Cast off.

TO MAKE UP
Join instep, top and back leg seams, leaving an opening. Sew in soles. Stuff and close opening. Join arm seams, leaving an opening. Stuff and close opening. Join centre seam on each body piece. Join body pieces together, leaving cast off edge open. Stuff and gather open edge, pull up and secure. Join sides of head from cast on edge to first marker. Sew in head gusset, placing point at centre front seam and cast on edge in line with second marker on sides of head. Join centre seams of back head, then sew to front head, matching markers and leaving cast on edge open. Stuff and gather open edge, pull up and secure. Sew head to body. Attach yarn about 1cm/½in below top of one arm, thread yarn through body at shoulder position, then attach other arm, pull yarn tightly and thread through body again in same place, then attach yarn to first arm again and fasten off. Attach legs at hip position in same way as arms. Join paired ear pieces together and sew

them in place. With Brown, embroider face features.

Jumper

FRONT

With 3¼mm (No 10/US 3) needles and A, cast on 25 sts. Beg with a k row, work 4 rows in st st.

1st rib row K1, [p1, k1] to end.
2nd rib row P1, [k1, p1] to end.
Beg with a k row, work 4 rows in st st.
Next row K6A, k 1st row of chart, k6A.
Next row P6A, p 2nd row of chart, p6A.
Work a further 2 rows as set. Mark each end of last row. Cont working from chart until 15th row of chart has been worked. Cont in A only, work 4 rows.

Shape Shoulders

Next row Cast off 6 sts, (1 st on needle), [p1, k1] 6 times, cast off rem 6 sts.

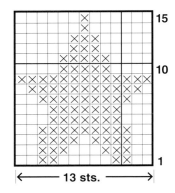

◄—— **13 sts.** ——►

☐ = **Navy (A)**

☒ = **Cream**

With right side facing, rejoin yarn to centre 13 sts, and rib 2 rows, inc one st at each end of every row. 17 sts. Beg with a k row, work 3 rows in st st. Cast off.

BACK

Work as given for Front, omitting "star" motif.

SLEEVES

Join shoulder and neckband seams, reversing seams on st st section of neckband.
With 3¼mm (No 10/US 3) needles, A and right side facing, k up 25 sts between markers. Beg with a p row, work 12 rows in st st. Work 3 rows in rib as given for Front. Cast off in rib.

TO MAKE UP

Join sleeve seams and side seams, reversing seams on first 4 rows.

Stars and Stripes Bear

See Page
25

MATERIALS

Bear 4 25g hanks of Rowan Lightweight DK in Brown (A).
Small amount of same in Black (B).
Pair of 2¾mm (No 12/US 2) knitting needles.
Stuffing.
Sweater
2 50g hanks of Rowan DK Tweed in main colour (C).
Small amount of Rowan Designer DK Wool in each of Cream, Navy and Red.
Pair each of 3¼mm (No 10/US 3) and 4 mm (No 8/US 6) knitting needles.

MEASUREMENTS

Bear approximately 32cm/12½in high.

TENSIONS

32 sts and 40 rows to 10cm/4in square over st st using Lightweight DK yarn and 2¾mm (No 12/US 2) needles.
22 sts and 30 rows to 10cm/4in square over st st using DK Tweed yarn and 4 mm (No 8/US 6) needles.

ABBREVIATIONS

See page 5.

NOTES

Read chart from right to left on right side (k) rows and from left to right on wrong side (p) rows. When working motif, use separate lengths of contrast colours for each coloured area and twist yarns together on wrong side at joins to avoid holes.

Bear

RIGHT LEG

With 2¾mm (No 12/US 2) needles and A, cast on 24 sts. P 1 row.
Next row K1, [m1, k2] to last st, m1, k1.
P 1 row.
Next row K9, [m1, k1] 3 times, [k1, m1] 3 times, k12, [m1, k1] 3 times, [k1, m1] 3 times, k3.

P 1 row.
Next row K12, [m1, k2] 4 times, k16, [m1, k2] 4 times, k4. 56 sts.
Work 13 rows in st st.
Next row K11, cast off next 12 sts, k to end.
Work across all sts.
Next row P30, p2 tog tbl, p2, p2 tog, p8.
Next row K7, k2 tog, k2, skpo, k16, skpo, k1, k2 tog, k8.

Next row P7, p2 tog, p1, p2 tog tbl, p26. 36 sts.
** Work 6 rows. Inc one st at each end of next row and 2 foll 4th rows. 42 sts. Work 13 rows.
Next row K8, k2 tog, k1, skpo, k16, k2 tog, k1, skpo, k8.
Work 3 rows.
Next row K7, k2 tog, k1, skpo, k14, k2 tog, k1, skpo, k7.
Work 1 row.
Next row K6, k2 tog, k1, skpo, k12, k2 tog, k1, skpo, k6.
Work 1 row.
Next row K5, k2 tog, k1, skpo, k10, k2 tog, k1, skpo, k5.
Work 1 row.
Next row K4, k2 tog, k1, skpo, k8, k2 tog, k1, skpo, k4.
Next row P3, p2 tog tbl, p1, p2 tog, p6, p2 tog tbl, p1, p2 tog, p3.
Next row K2, k2 tog, k1, skpo, k4, k2 tog, k1, skpo, k2. 14 sts.
Cast off.

LEFT LEG

With 2¾mm (No 12/US 2) needles and A, cast on 24 sts. P 1 row.
Next row K1, [m1, k2] to last st, m1, k1.
P 1 row.
Next row K3, [m1, k1] 3 times, [k1, m1] 3 times, k12, [m1, k1] 3 times, [k1, m1] 3 times, k9.
P 1 row.

Next row K6, [m1, k2] 4 times, k16, [m1, k2] 4 times, k10. 56 sts.
Work 13 rows in st st.
Next row K33, cast off next 12 sts, k to end.
Work across all sts.
Next row P8, p2 tog tbl, p2, p2 tog, p30.
Next row K8, skpo, k1, k2 tog, k16, k2 tog, k2, skpo, k7.
Next row P26, p2 tog, p1, p2 tog tbl, p7. 36 sts.
Complete as Right Leg from ** to end.

ARMS (MAKE 2)
With 2¾mm (No 12/US 2) needles and A, cast on 15 sts. P 1 row.
Next row K1, [m1, k2] to end. 22 sts.
Beg with a p row, work in st st, inc one st at each end of 4 foll alt rows, then on every foll 4th row until there are 40 sts.
Work 19 rows straight.
Next row K7, k2 tog, k2, skpo, k14, k2 tog, k2, skpo, k7.
Work 3 rows.
Next row K6, k2 tog, k2, skpo, k12, k2 tog, k2, skpo, k6.
Work 1 row.
Next row K5, k2 tog, k2, skpo, k10, k2 tog, k2, skpo, k5.
Work 1 row.
Next row K4, k2 tog, k2, skpo, k8, k2 tog, k2, skpo, k4.
Next row P3, p2 tog tbl, p2, p2 tog, p6, p2 tog tbl, p2, p2 tog, p3.
Next row K2, k2 tog, k2, skpo, k4, k2 tog, k2, skpo, k2. 16 sts.
Cast off.

BODY
Begin at neck edge.
With 2¾mm (No 12/US 2) needles and A, cast on 24 sts. P 1 row.
Next row K1, [m1, k2] to last st, m1, k1.
P 1 row.
Next row K2, [m1, k3] to last st, m1, k1. 48 sts.
Work 7 rows in st st.
Next row K10, m1, k1, m1, k2, m1, k1, m1, k9, m1, k2, m1, k9, m1, k1, m1, k2, m1, k1, m1, k10.
Work 5 rows.
Next row K11, [m1, k2] 4 times, k9, m1, k2, m1, k11, [m1, k2] 4 times, k9.
P 1 row.
Next row K12, m1, k3, m1, k2, m1, k3, m1, k28, m1, k3, m1, k2, m1, k3, m1, k12. 76 sts.
Work 5 rows.
Next row K17, m1, k2, m1, k38, m1, k2, m1, k17.
Work 5 rows.
Next row K18, m1, k2, m1, k40, m1, k2, m1, k18.
Work 5 rows.
Next row K19, m1, k2, m1, k42, m1, k2, m1, k19. 88 sts.

Work 19 rows.
Next row K18, k2 tog, k2, skpo, k40, k2 tog, k2, skpo, k18.
P 1 row.
Next row K17, k2 tog, k2, skpo, k38, k2 tog, k2, skpo, k17.
P 1 row.
Next row K16, k2 tog, k2, skpo, k36, k2 tog, k2, skpo, k16.
P 1 row.
Next row K10, k2 tog, k3, k2 tog, k2, skpo, k3, skpo, k24, k2 tog, k3, k2 tog, k2, skpo, k3, skpo, k10.
P 1 row.
Next row K9, [k2 tog, k2] twice, [skpo, k2] twice, k6, skpo, k2, k2 tog, k8, [k2 tog, k2] twice, [skpo, k2] twice, k7.
P 1 row.
Next row K8, [k2 tog, k1] twice, [k1, skpo] twice, k6, skpo, k2, k2 tog, k6, [k2 tog, k1] twice, [k1, skpo] twice, k8.
P 1 row.
Next row K1, [k2 tog, k2] 3 times, [skpo, k2] 3 times, [k2 tog, k2] 3 times, [skpo, k2] twice, skpo, k1.
P 1 row.
Next row [K2 tog, k1] to end. 24 sts.
Cast off.

HEAD
Begin at neck edge.
With 2¾mm (No 12/US 2) needles and A, cast on 24 sts. Beg with a k row, work 4 rows in st st.
Next row K1, [m1, k2] to last st, m1, k1.
Work 3 rows.
Next row K2, [m1, k3] to last st, m1, k1.
Work 3 rows.
Next row Cast on 4, k7, [m1, k4] to last st, m1, k1.
Cast on 4 sts at beg of next 5 rows. 84 sts. Work 14 rows. Mark each end of last row. Cast off 9 sts at beg of next 2 rows. Dec one st at each end of next 5 rows, then on 3 foll alt rows. 50 sts. P 1 row.
Next row K18, [skpo, k2] twice, [k2 tog, k2] twice, k3, skpo, turn.
Next row Sl 1, p20, p2 tog, turn.
Next row Sl 1, k20, skpo, turn.
Rep last 2 rows 3 times more, then work 1st of the 2 rows again.
Next row Sl 1, k20, sl 1, k2 tog, psso, turn.
Next row Sl 1, p20, p3 tog, turn.
Next row Sl 1, k20, skpo, turn.
Next row Sl 1, p20, p2 tog, turn.
Rep last 2 rows 4 times more. Work on rem 22 sts for gusset. Dec one st at each end of 5th row and foll 4th row, then on 2 foll alt rows. P 1 row.
Next row K2 tog, k2, skpo, [k2, k2 tog] twice. 10 sts.
Work 7 rows. Dec one st at each end of every row until 2 sts rem. Work 2 tog and fasten off.

EARS (MAKE 4)
With 2¾mm (No 12/US 2) needles and A, cast on 20 sts. Work in st st, dec one st at each end of 7th row, foll 4th row, then on 2 foll alt rows. Dec one st at each end of next row. 10 sts. Cast off.

NOSE
With 2¾mm (No 12/US 2) needles and B, cast on 9 sts. Work in st st, dec one st at each end of 3rd row and 2 foll alt rows. Work 1 row. Work 3 tog and fasten off.

TO MAKE UP
Join instep, top and inner seams of legs, leaving cast on edge free. Stuff and join sole seams. Join top and underarm seams of arms, leaving an opening. Stuff and close opening. Fold sides of body to centre and join cast off edge together, then join back seam. Stuff and gather open edge, pull up and secure. Join underchin and snout seam of head from cast on edge to markers. Sew in gusset. Stuff and gather open edge, pull up and secure. Sew head to body.
Attach yarn approximately 1cm/⅜in below top of one arm, thread through body at shoulder position, then attach other arm, pull up yarn tightly and thread through body again in same place, then attach yarn to first arm again and fasten off. Attach legs at hip position in same way as arms. Join paired ear pieces together and sew them in place. Sew on nose. With Black, embroider mouth and eyes.

Sweater

FRONT
With 3¼mm (No 10/US 3) needles and C, cast on 46 sts. Beg with a k row, work 4 rows in st st.
1st rib row K2, [p2, k2] to end.
2nd rib row P2, [k2, p2] to end.
Rep last 2 rows once more.
Change to 4 mm (No 8/US 6) needles. Beg with a k row, work 10 rows in st st.
Next row K10C, k across 1st row of chart, k10C.
Next row P10C, p across 2nd row of chart, p10C.
Work a further 18 rows as set. Cont in C only, work 14 rows.
Shape Shoulders and Neckband
Next row Cast off 8, k1 st more, [p2, k2] 7 times, cast off last 8 sts.
Change to 3¼mm (No 10/US 3) needles and with wrong side facing, rejoin yarn to centre 30 sts. Cont in rib, inc one st at each end of 5 foll alt rows. 40 sts. Rib 1 row. Cast off in rib.

BACK

Using C throughout, work as given for Front.

SLEEVES

Join shoulder and neckband seams.
Place markers at side edges 30 rows down from shoulder seams on Back and Front. With 4 mm (No 8/US 6) needles, C and right side facing, k up 52 sts between markers.
Beg with a p row, work in st st, dec one st at each end of 2nd row and 3 foll 4th rows. 44 sts. Work 1 row.
Dec row K3, [k2 tog, k2] to last st, k1. 34 sts.
Change to 3¼mm (No 10/US 3) needles.
Work 4 rows in rib as given for Front.
Beg with a p row, work 4 rows in st st.
Cast off.

TO MAKE UP

Join side and sleeve seams.

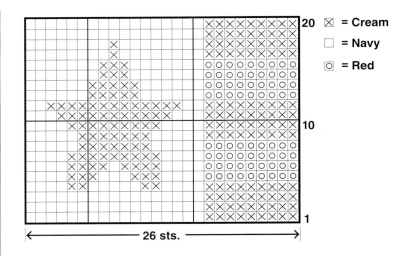

☒ = Cream
☐ = Navy
◉ = Red

French Bear

See Page
26

MATERIALS

Bear 4 50g balls of Rowan Designer DK Wool in Gold (A).
Small amount of same in Black (B).
Pair of 3¼mm (No 10/US 3) knitting needles.
Stuffing.
Outfit 4 25g hanks of Rowan Lightweight DK in Navy (C).
1 hank of same in White (D).
1 50g ball of Rowan Designer DK Wool in Red (E).
Pair each of 3¼mm (No 10/US 3), 3¾ mm (No 9/US 4) and 4 mm (No 8/US 6) knitting needles.
Length of 1cm/⅜in wide elastic.

MEASUREMENTS

Bear approximately 41cm/16in high.

TENSIONS

26 sts and 50 rows to 10cm/4in square over garter st (every row k) using Designer DK yarn and 3¼mm (No 10/US 3) needles.
25 sts and 33 rows to 10cm/4in square over st st using Lightweight DK yarn and 3¾mm (No 9/US 4) needles.

ABBREVIATIONS

See page 5.

Bear

RIGHT LEG

With 3¼mm (No 10/US 3) needles and A, cast on 26 sts. K 1 row.
Next row K1, [m1, k2] to last st, m1, k1.
K 1 row.
Next row K5, [m1, k2] 5 times, k10, [m1, k2] 5 times, k4.
K 1 row.
Next row K6, [m1, k3] 5 times, k9, [m1, k3] 5 times, k4. 59 sts.
K 15 rows. **

Next row K12, [skpo] 3 times, [k2 tog] 3 times, k35.
K 1 row.
Next row K9, [skpo] 3 times, [k2 tog] 3 times, k17, skpo, [k2 tog] twice, k9.
K 1 row.
Next row K8, [skpo] twice, [k2 tog] twice, k28. 40 sts.
*** Cont in garter st, inc one st at each end of 6th row and 3 foll 4th rows. 48 sts. K 12 rows.
Next row K9, k2 tog, k2, skpo, k18, k2 tog, k2, skpo, k9.
K 3 rows.

Next row K8, k2 tog, k2, skpo, k16, k2 tog, k2, skpo, k8.
K 1 row.
Next row K7, k2 tog, k2, skpo, k14, k2 tog, k2, skpo, k7.
Cont in this way, dec 4 sts as set on 4 foll alt rows. 20 sts. K 1 row. Cast off.
Join all seams, leaving an opening.
Stuff and close opening.

LEFT LEG

Work as given for Right Leg to **.
Next row K35, [skpo] 3 times, [k2 tog] 3 times, k12.
K 1 row.
Next row K9, [skpo] twice, k2 tog, k17, [skpo] 3 times, [k2 tog] 3 times, k9.
K 1 row.
Next row K28, [skpo] twice, [k2 tog] twice, k8. 40 sts.
Complete as Right Leg from *** to end.

BODY

Begin at neck edge.
With 3¼mm (No 10/US 3) needles and A, cast on 17 sts. K 1 row.
Next row [K twice in next st] to end. 34 sts.
K 1 row.
Next row K4, [k twice in next st] to last 4 sts, k4. 60 sts.
K 15 rows.
Next row K13, [k twice in next st] 4 times, k26, [k twice in next st] 4 times, k13.

K 3 rows.
Next row K14, [k twice in next st, k1, k twice in next st] twice, k28, [k twice in next st, k1, k twice in next st] twice, k14.
K 3 rows.
Next row K16, [k twice in next st, k1] 4 times, k29, [k twice in next st, k1] 4 times, k15.
K 3 rows.
Next row K17, [k twice in next st, k2, k twice in next st, k1] twice, k31, [k twice in next st, k2, k twice in next st, k1] twice, k16. 92 sts.
K 37 rows.
Next row K17, [skpo, k2, skpo, k1] twice, k31, [k2 tog, k2, k2 tog, k1] twice, k16.
K 3 rows.
Next row K16, [skpo, k1] 4 times, k29, [k2 tog, k1] 4 times, k15.
K 3 rows.
Next row K14, [skpo, k1, skpo] twice, k28, [k2 tog, k1, k2 tog] twice, k14.
* **Next 2 rows** K12, sl 1, yf, turn, sl 1, k12.
K 1 row. * Rep from * to * twice, then work the 2 turning rows again.
Next row K13, [skpo] 4 times, k26, [k2 tog] 4 times, k13.
Rep from * to * once, then work the 2 turning rows again.
Next row K12, [skpo] 4 times, k20, [k2 tog] 4 times, k12.
K 1 row.
Next row K10, [skpo] 4 times, k16, [k2 tog] 4 times, k10.
K 1 row.
Next row K8, [skpo] 4 times, k12, [k2 tog] 4 times, k8.
Next row [K2 tog] to end. 18 sts.
Cast off.

ARMS (MAKE 2)

With $3\frac{1}{4}$mm (No 10/US 3) needles and A, cast on 7 sts. K 1 row.
Next row K1, [m1, k1] to end
Rep last 2 rows once more. 25 sts. K 1 row.
Next row K6, m1, k1, m1, k11, m1, k1, m1, k6.
K 1 row.
Next row K7, m1, k1, m1, k13, m1, k1, m1, k7.
K 1 row.
Next row K8, m1, k1, m1, k15, m1, k1, m1, k8. 37 sts.
K 10 rows.
Next row K1, [k2 tog, k2] to end. 28 sts.
K 3 rows.
Next row K1, [m1, k3] to end. 37 sts.
Cont in garter st, inc one st at each end of 3rd row and 3 foll 4th rows. 45 sts. K 16 rows.
Next row K8, k2 tog, k2, skpo, k17, k2 tog, k2, skpo, k8.
K 3 rows.
Next row K7, k2 tog, k2, skpo, k15, k2 tog, k2, skpo, k7.
K 1 row.
Next row K6, k2 tog, k2, skpo, k13, k2 tog, k2, skpo, k6.
Cont in this way, dec 4 sts as set on 4 foll alt rows. 17 sts. K 1 row. Cast off.
Join seam, leaving an opening. Stuff and close opening.

HEAD

Begin at snout.
With $3\frac{1}{4}$mm (No 10/US 3) needles and A, cast on 8 sts. K 1 row.
Next row K1, [m1, k1] to end.
Rep last 2 rows once more. 29 sts.
5th row and 5 foll alt rows K.
6th row K1, [m1, k13, m1, k1] twice.
8th row K1, [m1, k15, m1, k1] twice.
10th row K1, m1, k16, m1, k3, m1, k16, m1, k1.
12th row K1, m1, k17, m1, k5, m1, k17, m1, k1.
14th row K1, m1, k18, m1, k7, m1, k18, m1, k1.
16th row K1, m1, k19, m1, k9, m1, k19, m1, k1. 53 sts.
17th and 18th rows K.
19th row K2, [skpo, k1] 7 times, k8, [k2 tog, k1] 7 times, k1.
20th row K7, [m1, k4] 3 times, k1, [k4, m1] 3 times, k7.
K 3 rows.
24th row K7, [m1, k5] 3 times, k1, [k5, m1] 3 times, k7.
K 3 rows.
28th row K7, [m1, k6] 3 times, k1, [k6, m1] 3 times, k7.
K 3 rows.
Cont in this way, inc 6 sts as set on next row and 3 foll alt rows. 81 sts. K 1 row.
Next row K5, [m1, k4] 7 times, k15, [k4, m1] 7 times, k5. 95 sts.
K 20 rows.
Next row [K10, k2 tog] 7 times, k11.
K 3 rows.
Next row [K9, k2 tog] 8 times.
K 3 rows.
Next row [K8, k2 tog] 8 times.
K 3 rows.
Next row [K7, k2 tog] 8 times.
K 3 rows.
Cont in this way, dec 8 sts as set on next row and 5 foll alt rows. 16 sts. K 1 row.
Next row [K2 tog] 8 times.
Break off yarn. Thread end through rem sts, pull up and secure. Join seam, leaving an opening. Stuff and close opening.

EARS (MAKE 2)

With $3\frac{1}{4}$mm (No 10/US 3) needles and A, cast on 5 sts. K 1 row.
Next row K1, [m1, k1] to end.
K 1 row.
Next row K1, [m1, k3, m1, k1] twice.
K 1 row.
Next row K1, m1, k4, m1, k3, m1, k4, m1, k1.
K 1 row.
Next row K1, m1, [k5, m1] 3 times, k1. 21 sts.
K 15 rows.
Next row K1, skpo, k3, skpo, k5, k2 tog, k3, k2 tog, k1.
K 1 row.
Next row K1, skpo, k2, skpo, k3, k2 tog, k2, k2 tog, k1.
K 1 row.
Next row K1, [skpo, k1] twice, [k2 tog, k1] twice.
K 1 row.
Next row K1, skpo, sl 1, k2 tog, psso, k2 tog, k1.
Cast off.

NOSE

With $3\frac{1}{4}$mm (No 10/US 3) needles and B, cast on 9 sts. K 3 rows.
Next row K1, skpo, k3, k2 tog, k1.
K 1 row.
Next row K1, skpo, k1, k2 tog, k1.
K 1 row.
Next row K1, sl 1, k2 tog, psso, k1.
K 1 row. K3 tog and fasten off.

TO MAKE UP

Join back seam of body, then cast off edge. Stuff. Gather neck edge, pull up and secure. Sew head in position. Attach yarn at seam 1cm/$\frac{1}{4}$in below top of one arm, thread through body at shoulder position, then attach other arm, pull up yarn tightly and thread through body again in same place, attach to first arm again and fasten off. Attach legs at hip position in same way as arms. Sew on nose and embroider face features with Black. Fold ears in half widthwise and stitch together open edge. Sew ears in place.

Sweater

BACK AND FRONT ALIKE

With $3\frac{3}{4}$mm (No 9/US 4) needles and C, cast on 53 sts.
1st rib row K1, [p1, k1] to end.
2nd rib row P1, [k1, p1] to end.
Beg with a k row, work in st st and stripe patt of 2 rows D and 2 rows C until 24 rows have been worked. Mark each end of last row. Patt 31 rows more. Cont in C only. Beg with a 2nd row, work 4 rows in rib. Cast off in rib.

SLEEVES

Overlap rib sections of Back and Front at shoulders and secure at side edges.
With $3\frac{3}{4}$mm (No 9/US 4) needles, C and right side facing, k up 53 sts between

markers. P 1 row. Work in st st and stripe patt as given for Back and Front, dec one st at each end of every 3rd row until 45 sts rem. Work 3 rows. Cont in C only. Beg with a 2nd row, work 2 rows in rib as given for Back and Front. Cast off in rib.

TO MAKE UP
Join side and sleeve seams.

Trousers

TO MAKE
With 3¾mm (No 9/US 4) needles and C, cast on 53 sts. K 7 rows.
Beg with a k row, work in st st for 14cm/ 5½in, ending with a p row.
1st rib row K1, [p1, k1] to end.
2nd rib row P1, [k1, p1] to end.
Rib 6 rows more. Cast off. Make one more.
Beginning at ribbed top, join centre back

and front seams for 13cm/5in, then join leg seams. Join waist length of elastic into ring. Place along wrong side of rib and work herring bone casing over it.

Beret

TO MAKE
With 3¼mm (No 10/US 3) needles and C, cast on 64 sts. K 5 rows.
Next row K5, [m1, k1, m1, k8] 6 times, m1, k1, m1, k4.
K 5 rows.
Next row K6, [m1, k1, m1, k10] 6 times, m1, k1, m1, k5.
K 5 rows.
Cont in this way, inc 14 sts as set on next row and foll 6th row. 120 sts. K 4 rows.
Next row K7, [k2tog, k1, k2 tog, k12] 6 times, k2 tog, k1, k2 tog, k6.
K 3 rows.

Next row K6, [k2 tog, k1, k2 tog, k10] 6 times, k2 tog, k1, k2 tog, k5.
K 3 rows.
Cont in this way, dec 14 sts as set on next row and every foll 4th row until 22 sts rem. K 1 row.
Next row [K2 tog] to end.
Next row K1, [k2 tog] to end.
Break off yarn. Thread end through rem sts, pull up and secure. Join seam.

Scarf

TO MAKE
With 4 mm (No 8/US 6) needles and E, cast on 3 sts. K 1 row. Work in garter st, inc one st at each end of next row and every foll alt row until there are 43 sts, then on every row until there are 77 sts. K 1 row. Cast off.

Small Bear in Sweater

See Page 27

MATERIALS
Bear 1 50g ball of Rowan Designer DK Wool.
Oddment of Black yarn for embroidery.
Pair of 3¼mm (No 10/US 3) knitting needles.
Stuffing.
Sweater 1 100g hank of Rowan Magpie Tweed or Designer DK used double.
Pair of 6½ mm (No 3/US 10) needles.

MEASUREMENTS
Bear approximately 18cm/7in high.

TENSIONS
28 sts and 36 rows to 10cm/4in square over st st using DK yarn and 3¼mm (No 10/US 3) needles.
15 sts and 23 rows to 10cm/4in square over st st using chunky yarn and 6½ mm (No 3/US 10) needles.

ABBREVIATIONS
See page 5.

Bear

RIGHT LEG
With 3¼mm (No 10/US 3) needles cast on 10 sts. P 1 row.
Next row K1, [m1, k1] to end.
P 1 row.
Next row K7, m1, k1, m1, k8, m1, k1, m1, k2. 23 sts.
Work 3 rows in st st.
Next row K4, [skpo] twice, [k2 tog] twice, k11.
Next row P9, [p2 tog] twice, [p2 tog tbl] twice, p2.
Next row K3, k2 tog, k10. 14 sts.

** Work 11 rows, inc one st at each end of 4th row. 16 sts.
Next row K1, k2 tog, k1, skpo, k3, k2 tog, k1, skpo, k2.
P 1 row.
Next row [K2 tog, k1, skpo, k1] twice.
Next row [P2 tog] to end.
Break off yarn. Thread end through rem sts, pull up and secure. Join all seams, leaving an opening. Stuff and close opening.

LEFT LEG
With 3¼mm (No 10/US 3) needles cast on 10 sts. P 1 row.
Next row K1, [m1, k1] to end.

P 1 row.
Next row K2, m1, k1, m1, k8, m1, k1, m1, k7. 23 sts.
Work 3 rows in st st.
Next row K11, [skpo] twice, [k2 tog] twice, k4.
Next row P2, [p2 tog] twice, [p2 tog tbl] twice, p9.
Next row K10, skpo, k3. 14 sts.
Complete as given for Right Leg from ** to end.

BODY
Begin at neck edge.
With 3¼mm (No 10/US 3) needles cast on 15 sts. P 1 row.
Next row K1, [m1, k1] to end. 29 sts.
Beg with a p row, work 5 rows in st st.
Next row [K7, m1] twice, k1, [m1, k7] twice.
Work 3 rows.
Next row K16, m1, k1, m1, k16. 35 sts.
Work 5 rows.
Next row K15, skpo, k1, k2 tog, k15.
Work 3 rows.
Next row K14, skpo, k1, k2 tog, k14.
Work 3 rows.
Next row K1, [k2 tog] to end. 16 sts.
P 1 row. Cast off.

ARMS (MAKE 2)
With 3¼mm (No 10/US 3) needles cast on 6 sts. P 1 row.
Next row K1, [m1, k1] to end.

P 1 row.
Next row K1, [m1, k4, m1, k1] twice. 15 sts.
Work 3 rows in st st.
Next row K1, [skpo, k2, k2 tog, k1] twice.
Work 13 rows, inc one st at each end of
4th row. 13 sts.
Next row K1, [skpo, k1, k2 tog, k1] twice.
P 1 row.
Next row K1, [k2 tog] to end.
Break off yarn. Thread end through rem
sts, pull up and secure. Join seam,
leaving an opening. Stuff and close
opening.

HEAD
Begin at back.
With 3¼mm (No 10/US 3) needles cast
on 7 sts. P 1 row.
Next row K1, [m1, k1] to end.
Rep last 2 rows once more. 25 sts. Work
3 rows in st st.
Next row K1, [m1, k3] to end. 33 sts.
Work 13 rows.
Next row K1, [k2 tog] to end.
Work 3 rows.
Next row K1, [k2 tog] to end. 9 sts.
P 1 row. Break off yarn. Thread end
through rem sts, pull up and secure. Join
seam, leaving an opening. Stuff and

close opening.

EARS (MAKE 2)
With 3¼mm (No 10/US 3) needles cast
on 3 sts. P 1 row.
Next row K1, [m1, k1] to end.
Rep last 2 rows once more. 9 sts. P 1 row.
Next row K1, m1, k2, m1, k3, m1, k2,
m1, k1. 13 sts.
Work 5 rows in st st.
Next row [K1, skpo] twice, k1, [k2 tog,
k1] twice.
P 1 row.
Next row [Skpo] twice, k1, [k2 tog] twice.
P 1 row.
Next row Skpo, k1, k2 tog.
Cast off.

TO MAKE UP
Join back seam of body, then cast off
edge. Stuff. Gather neck edge, pull up
and secure. Sew head in place. Fold
ears in half widthwise and stitch together
open edge. Sew ears in place. With
Black, embroider face features. Attach
yarn at seam about 1cm/¼in below top of
one arm, thread through body at
shoulder position, then attach other arm,
pull yarn tightly and thread through body

again in same place, attach yarn to first
arm and fasten off. Attach legs at hip
position in same way as arms.

Sweater

BACK AND FRONT ALIKE
With 6½mm (No 3/US 10) needles cast on
14 sts. Work 2 rows in k1, p1 rib. Beg with
a k row, work 5 rows in st st. Mark each
end of last row. Work a further 7 rows.
Shape Shoulders
Next row Cast off 3 sts, (1 st on needle),
p1, [k1, p1] 3 times, cast off rem 3 sts.
With wrong side facing, rejoin yarn to
rem 8 sts, work twice in first st, rib to last
st, work twice in last st. Rib 3 rows more,
inc one st at each end of first row. 12 sts.
Cast off in rib.

SLEEVES
Join shoulder and neckband seams.
With 6½mm (No 3/US 10) needles and
right side facing, k up14 sts between
markers. Beg with a p row, work 3 rows
in st st. Work 2 rows in k1, p1 rib. Cast
off in rib.
Join side and sleeve seams.

Artist Bear

See Page
28

MATERIALS
Bear 4 25g hanks of Rowan
Lightweight DK.
Small amount of Black yarn for
embroidery.
Pair of 2¾mm (No 12/US 2) knitting
needles.
Stuffing.
Outfit 3 50 balls of Rowan Cotton
Glace in Cream (A).
2 25g hanks of Rowan Lightweight DK
in Black (B).
Small amount of 4 ply yarn in each of
Red (C) and Cream.
Pair each of 3¼mm (No 10/US 3) and
3¾mm (No 9/US 4) knitting needles.
70cm/27½in of 20cm/8in wide soft

black fabric for bow.

MEASUREMENTS
Bear approximately 36cm/14in high.

TENSIONS
32 sts and 40 rows to 10cm/4in
square over st st using Lightweight
DK yarn and 2¾mm (No 12/US 2)
needles.
23 sts and 32 rows to 10cm/4in
square over st st on using Cotton
Glace yarn and 3¾mm (No 9/US 4)
needles.

ABBREVIATIONS
See page 5.

Work on this set of sts only. Dec one st at
beg of next row and 3 foll alt rows, then
at end of next row and at beg of foll row.
19 sts. Work 1 row. Break off yarn and
rejoin at inside edge to secend set of 25
sts, k to end. Dec one st at end of next
row and 3 foll alt rows, then at beg of
next row and at end of foll row. 19 sts.

Work 1 row. P 1 row across both set of
sts. 38 sts. Work 21 rows.
Next row P19, turn.
Work on this set of sts only. Dec one st at
each end of next row and 2 foll alt rows,
then on 2 foll rows. 9 sts. Work 1 row.
Cast off. Rejoin yarn to rem sts and
complete as first side.

SOLE (MAKE 2)
With 2¾mm (No 12/US 2) needles cast
on 5 sts. K 1 row. Cont in st st, inc one st
at each end of next 3 rows and foll alt
row, then on foll 4th row. 15 sts. Work 11
rows straight. Dec one st at each end of
next row, foll 4th row, and on foll alt row,
then at each end of next 2 rows. 5 sts.
Work 1 row. Cast off.

ARMS (MAKE 2)
* With 2¾mm (No 12/US 2) needles cast
on 8 sts. Beg with a k row, work 2 rows in
st st. Cont in st st, inc one st at each end
of next row and foll alt row. Work 1 row.*
Inc one st at beg of next row. Work 1
row. Inc one st at each end of foll row. 15
sts. Work 1 row. Break off yarn. Rep from
* to *. Inc one st at end of next row. Work

Bear

LEGS (MAKE 2)
With 2¾mm (No 12/US 2) needles cast
on 50 sts. Beg with a k row, work 10 rows
in st st.
Next row K25, turn.

1 row. Inc one st at each end of foll row. 15 sts. Work 1 row. K 1 row across both set of sts. 30 sts. Inc one st at each end of 2nd row and 3 foll 6th rows. 38 sts. Work 14 rows straight.
Next row P19, turn.
Work on this set of sts only. Dec one st at each end of next row and 2 foll alt rows, then on 2 foll rows. 9 sts. Work 1 row. Cast off. Rejoin yarn to rem sts and complete as first side.

BODY (MAKE 2)
* With $2\frac{3}{4}$mm (No 12/US 2) needles cast on 7 sts. K 1 row. Cont in st st, inc one st at each end of next 2 rows and 5 foll alt rows. 21 sts. Work 1 row.* Break off yarn. Rep from * to *. K 1 row across both set of sts. 42 sts. Work 25 rows straight. Dec one st at each end of next row, 2 foll 4th rows and 3 foll alt rows, then on every row until 20 sts rem. Work 1 row. Cast off.

BACK HEAD
With $2\frac{3}{4}$mm (No 12/US 2) needles cast on 7 sts. K 1 row. Cont in st st, inc one st at each end of next 2 rows, then at end of foll 5 rows. Work 1 row. Inc one st at beg of next 2 rows. 18 sts. Break off yarn.
With $2\frac{3}{4}$mm (No 12/US 2) needles cast on 7 sts. K 1 row. Cont in st st, inc one st at each end of next 2 rows, then at beg of foll 5 rows. Work 1 row. Inc one st at end of next 2 rows. 18 sts. P 1 row across both set of sts. 36 sts. Work 22 rows straight.
Next row K2 tog, k16, turn.
Work on this set of sts only. Dec one st at each end of 2 foll 3rd rows, then foll alt row. Mark beg of last row. Dec one st at end of next row, each end of foll row and at end of next row. 7 sts. Work 1 row. Cast off.
Rejoin yarn at inside edge to rem sts, k to last 2 sts, k2 tog. Dec one st at each end of 2 foll 3rd rows, then foll alt row. Mark end of last row. Dec one st at beg of next row, each end of foll row and at beg of foll row. 7 sts. Work 1 row. Cast off.

RIGHT SIDE HEAD
With $2\frac{3}{4}$mm (No 12/US 2) needles cast on 10 sts. K 1 row. P 1 row inc one st at beg. Cont in st st, inc one st at each end of next row and at beg of foll 6 rows, then at end of next row. Inc one st at each end of next row. Inc one st at end of next row and at same edge on foll 3 rows. 26 sts. Work 11 rows straight. Mark end of last row. Cast off 2 sts at beg of next row. Dec one st at end of next row and at same edge on foll 6 rows. Dec one st at each end of next row, then at end of foll row. Dec one st at each end of foll alt row. Work 1 row. Dec one st at end of next 3 rows. 9 sts. Work 1 row. Mark end of last row. Cast off.

LEFT SIDE HEAD
Work as given for Right Side Head, reversing shapings by reading p for k and k for p.

HEAD GUSSET
With $2\frac{3}{4}$mm (No 12/US 2) needles cast on 20 sts. Work 10 rows in st st. Dec one st at each end of next row and 3 foll 4th rows, then on 3 foll alt rows. Work 3 rows. Dec one st at each end of next 2 rows. Work 2 tog and fasten off.

EARS (MAKE 4)
With $2\frac{3}{4}$mm (No 12/US 2) needles cast on 13 sts. Work 5 rows in st st. Dec one st at each end of next row and 2 foll alt rows, then on foll 2 rows. 3 sts. Cast off.

TO MAKE UP
Join instep, top and back leg seams, leaving an opening. Sew in soles. Stuff and close opening. Join arm seams, leaving an opening. Stuff and close opening. Join centre seam on each body piece. Join body pieces together, leaving cast off edge open. Stuff and gather open edge, pull up and secure. Join sides of head from cast on edge to first marker. Sew in head gusset, placing point at centre front seam and cast on edge in line with second markers on sides of head. Join centre seams of back head, then sew to front head, matching markers and leaving cast on edge open. Stuff and gather open edge, pull up and secure. Sew head to body. Attach yarn about 1cm/$\frac{1}{4}$in below top of one arm, thread yarn through body at shoulder position, then attach other arm, pull yarn tightly and thread through body again in same place, then attach yarn to first arm again and fasten off. Attach legs at hip position in same way as arms. Join paired ear pieces together and sew them in place. With Black, embroider face features.

Smock

BACK
With $3\frac{3}{4}$mm (No 9/US 4) needles and A, cast on 69 sts. K 3 rows. Beg with a k row, work 34 rows in st st. Mark each end of last row. Work 13 rows.
Next row P1, [p2 tog] 3 times, *p3 tog, [p2 tog] 5 times; rep from * 3 times more, p3 tog, [p2 tog] 3 times, p1. 33 sts. Cast off.
With $3\frac{3}{4}$mm (No 9/US 4) needles, A and right side facing, k up 33 sts along cast off edge of back. Beg with a p row, work 9 rows in st st.
Shape Neck
Next row K12, cast off next 9 sts, k to end.
Work on last set of sts only. Dec one st at neck edge on next 2 rows. 10 sts. Work 1 row. Cast off.
With wrong side facing, rejoin yarn to rem sts and complete as first side.

LEFT FRONT
With $3\frac{3}{4}$mm (No 9/US 4) needles and A, cast on 39 sts. K 3 rows.
Next row (right side) K.
Next row K2, p to end.
Rep last 2 rows 16 times more. Mark side edge of last row. Work 7 rows.
Shape Neck
Cast off 2 sts at beg of next row. Dec one st at armhole edge on 3 foll right side rows. 34 sts.
Next row [P2 tog] 3 times, *p3 tog, [p2 tog] 3 times; rep from * twice more, p1. 16 sts. Cast off.
With $3\frac{3}{4}$mm (No 9/US 4) needles, A and right side facing, k up 16 sts along cast off edge of front. Beg with a p row, work in st st, dec one st at neck edge on 6 foll alt rows. 10 sts. Work 1 row. Cast off.

RIGHT FRONT
With $3\frac{3}{4}$mm (No 9/US 4) needles and A, cast on 39 sts. K 3 rows.
Next row (right side) K.
Next row P to last 2 sts, k2.
Complete as given for Left Front, reversing shapings.

SLEEVES
Join shoulder seams.
With $3\frac{3}{4}$mm (No 9/US 4) needles, A and right side facing, k up 42 sts between markers. Beg with a p row, work 20 rows in st st.
Next row P2, [p2 tog, p2] to end. 32 sts. Cast off.
With $3\frac{3}{4}$mm (No 9/US 4) needles, A and right side facing, k up 32 sts along cast off edge of sleeve. K 4 rows. Cast off.

COLLAR
With $3\frac{3}{4}$mm (No 9/US 4) needles, A and right side facing, k up 17 sts up right front neck, 17 sts around back neck and 17 sts down left front neck. 51 sts.
1st row (right side) K to end.
2nd row K2, p to last 2 sts, k2.
Work a further 2 rows.
Next row K18, [m1, k3] 6 times, k to end.
Work 3 rows.
Next row K18, [m1, k4] twice, m1, k5, m1, [k4, m1] twice, k to end.
Work 3 rows.
Next row K18, [m1, k5] twice, m1, k7,

m1, [k5, m1] twice, k to end.
Work 4 rows. K 2 rows. Cast off.

POCKETS (MAKE 2)
WIth 3¾mm (No 9/US 4) needles and A,
cast on 11 sts. Beg with a k row, work 11
rows in st st. K 2 rows. Cast off.

HANKIE
With 3¼mm (No 10/US 3) needles and
C, cast on 19 sts. K 3 rows.
1st row K.
2nd row K2, p15, k2.
Rep last 2 rows 8 times more. K 3 rows.
Cast off.

TO MAKE UP
Join side and sleeve seams. Sew on
pockets. Fold fabric in half lengthwise
(right side inside) and joim seam all
round, leaving an opening. Turn to right

side and close opening. With Cream,
embroider spots on hankie.

Beret

TO MAKE
With 3¾mm (No 9/US 4) needles and B,
cast on 57 sts. K 7 rows.
Next row K1, [k twice in next st, k1] to
end. 85 sts.
Beg with a p row, work 3 rows in st st.
Next row K1, [m1, k4] to end.
Work 3 rows.
Next row K1, [m1, k5] to end.
Work 3 rows.
Next row K1, [m1, k6] to end.
Work 3 rows.
Next row K1, [m1, k7] to end. 169 sts.
Work 4 rows.
Next row [P19, p2 tog tbl] to last st, p1.

Next row K1, [skpo, k8] to end.
Work 2 rows.
Next row [P7, p2 tog tbl] to last st, p1.
Work 2 rows.
Next row K1, [skpo, k6] to end.
Work 2 rows.
Next row [P5, p2 tog tbl] to last st, p1.
Cont in this way, dec 16 sts as set on
every 3rd row until 33 sts rem.
Work 2 rows.
Next row K1, [skpo] to end.
Next row [P2 tog tbl] to last st, p1.
Break off yarn, thread end through rem
sts, pull up and secure. Join seam.
With 3¾mm (No 9/US 4) needles and
using two strands of B yarn together,
cast on 5 sts for stalk. Work 5 rows in st
st. Cast off. Join cast on and cast off
edges together and sew to top of beret.

Ballerina Bear

See Page

29

MATERIALS
Bear 2 25g hanks of Rowan
Lightweight DK.
Small amount of Brown yarn for
embroidery.
Pair of 2¾mm (No 12/US 2) knitting
needles.
Stuffing.
Outfit 1 50g ball of Rowan True 4 ply
Botany.
Pair of 2¾mm (No 12/US 2) knitting
needles.
Medium size crochet hook.
Approximately 13cm/5in of

122cm/60in wide net fabric.

MEASUREMENTS
Bear approximately 18cm/7in high.

TENSION
32 sts and 40 rows to 10cm/4in
square over st st using DK or 4 ply
yarn and 2¾mm (No 12/US 2)
needles.

ABBREVIATIONS
See page 5.

Bear

LEGS (MAKE 2)
With 2¾mm (No 12/US 2) needles cast
on 26 sts. Beg with a k row, work 5 rows
in st st.
Next row P13, turn.
Work on this first set of sts only. Dec
st at beg of next row and foll alt row, then
at end of foll row. 10 sts. Break off yarn
and rejoin at inside edge to second set
of 13 sts, p to end. Dec one st at end of
next row and foll alt row, then at beg of
foll row. 10 sts. K 1 row across both sets
of sts. 20 sts. Work 10 rows.
Next row P10, turn.
Work on this set of sts only. Dec one st at

each end of next 2 rows. 6 sts. Work 1
row. Cast off. Rejoin yarn to rem sts and
complete as first side.

SOLES (MAKE 2)
With 2¾mm (No 12/US 2) needles cast
on 3 sts. K 1 row. Cont in st st, inc one st
at each end of next 2 rows and foll alt
row. 9 sts. Work 6 rows straight. Dec
one st at each end of next row and foll
alt row, then on foll row. 3 sts. P 1 row.
Cast off.

ARMS (MAKE 2)
* With 2¾mm (No 12/US 2) needles cast
on 4 sts. Beg with a k row, work in st st,
inc one st at each end of 3rd row and foll
alt row. 8 sts. P 1 row.* Break off yarn.

Work from * to *. K 1 row across both
sets of sts. 16 sts. Inc one st at each end
of 2nd row and foll 4th row. 20 sts. Work
9 rows straight.
Next row K10, turn.
Work on this set of sts only. Dec one st at
each end of next 2 rows. 6 sts. Work 1
row. Cast off. Rejoin yarn to rem sts and
complete as first side.

BODY (MAKE 2)
* With 2¾mm (No 12/US 2) needles cast
on 3 sts. K 1 row. Cont in st st, inc one st
at each end of next 2 rows and 2 foll alt
rows. 11 sts.* Break off yarn. Work from *
to *. P 1 row across both sets of sts. 22
sts. Work 12 rows straight. Dec one st at
each end of next row and 2 foll 3rd rows,
then on foll alt row. 14 sts. P 1 row. Cast
off.

BACK HEAD
With 2¾mm (No 12/US 2) needles cast
on 3 sts. K 1 row. Cont in st st, inc one st
at each end of next 2 rows, then at end
of 3 foll rows. Work 1 row. Inc one st at
beg of next row. 11 sts. K1 row. Break off
yarn.
With 2¾mm (No 12/US 2) needles cast
on 3 sts. K 1 row. Cont in st st, inc one st
at each end of next 2 rows, then at beg
of 3 foll rows. Work 1 row. Inc one st at
end of next row. 11 sts. K 1 row. P 1 row
across both sets of sts. 22 sts. Work 6
rows straight.
Next row K11, turn.

Work on this set of sts only. Dec one st at each end of next row. Work 1 row. Dec one st at end of next 3 rows. Mark end of last row. Dec one st at each end of next row. 4 sts. Work 1 row. Cast off.
Rejoin yarn at inside edge to rem sts and k to end. Dec one st at each end of next row. Work 1 row. Dec one st at beg of next 3 rows. Mark beg of last row. Dec one st at each end of next row. 4 sts. Work 1 row. Cast off.

RIGHT SIDE HEAD
With 2¾mm (No 12/US 2) needles cast on 6 sts. K 1 row. P 1 row, inc one st at beg. Cont in st st, inc one st at each end of next row, then at beg of foll 4 rows. Inc one st at end of next row and at beg of foll row. 15 sts. Work 5 rows straight. Mark end of last row. Cast off 2 sts at beg of next row. Dec one st at end of next row and at beg of foll row. * Dec one st at each end of next row and at beg of foll row.* Rep from * to *. 5 sts. Work 1 row. Mark beg of last row. Cast off.

LEFT SIDE HEAD
Work as given for Right Side Head, reversing shapings by reading p for k and k for p.

HEAD GUSSET
With 2¾mm (No 12/US 2) needles cast on 11 sts. Beg with a k row, work 4 rows in st st. Dec one st at each end of next row and foll alt row, then on foll row. Work 2 rows. Dec one st at each end of next row. Work 1 row. K3 tog and fasten off.

EARS (MAKE 4)
With 2¾mm (No 12/US 2) needles cast on 6 sts. Work 3 rows in st st. Dec one st at each end of next 2 rows. Cast off.

TO MAKE UP
Join instep, top and back leg seams, leaving an opening. Sew in soles. Stuff and close opening. Join arm seams, leaving an opening. Stuff and close opening. Join centre seam on each body

piece. Join body pieces together, leaving cast off edge open. Stuff and gather open edge, pull up and secure. Join sides of head from cast on edge to first marker. Sew in head gusset, placing point at centre front seam and cast on edge in line with second marker on sides of head. Join centre seams of back head, then sew to front head, matching markers and leaving cast on edge open. Stuff and gather open edge, pull up and secure. Sew head to body. Attach yarn about 1cm/¼in below top of one arm, thread yarn through body at shoulder position, then attach other arm, pull yarn tightly and thread through body again in same place, then attach yarn to first arm again and fasten off. Attach legs at hip position in same way as arms. Join paired ear pieces together and sew them in place. With Brown, embroider face features.

Wrap-over Cardigan

BACK AND FRONTS
With 2¾mm (No 12/US 2) needles cast on 28 sts. K 5 rows. Beg with a k row, work 6 rows in st st. Mark each end of last row. Work a further 14 rows.
Shape Neck
Next row K9, cast off next 10 sts, k to end.
Work on last set of sts only for Left Front. Work 2 rows.
Next row P to last 2 sts, k2.
Next row K2, yf, k to end.
Next row P to last 3 sts, p1 tbl, yon, k2.
Next row K2, yf, k1 tbl, k to end.
Rep last 2 rows 5 times more. Mark side edge of last row. Cont inc at front edge as before until there are 28 sts.
Next row K to last 3 sts, k1 tbl, k2. K2 rows.
Next row Cast on 25 sts for tie, k to end. Cast off.
With wrong side facing, rejoin yarn to rem sts for Right Front and work 2 rows.

Next row K2, p to end.
Next row K to last 2 sts, yf, k2.
Next row K2, yrn, p1 tbl, p to end.
Next row K to last 3 sts, k1 tbl, yf, k2.
Rep last 2 rows 5 times more. Mark side edge of last row. Cont inc at front edge as before until there are 28 sts.
Next row K2, k1 tbl, k to end. K 1 row.
Next row Cast on 25 sts for tie, k to end. K 1 row. Cast off.

SLEEVES
With 2¾mm (No 12/US 2) needles and right side facing, k up 28 sts between markers. Beg with a p row, work 15 rows in st st, dec one st at each end of every 4th row. 22 sts.
Next row K10, k2 tog, k10.
K 2 rows. Cast off.

TO MAKE UP
Join side and sleeve seams.

Shoes

TO MAKE
With 2¾mm (No 12/US 2) needles and using two strands of yarn together, cast on 12 sts. P 1 row.
Next row K1, [m1, k1] to end.
P 1 row.
Next row K1, m1, k8, [m1, k1] 6 times, k7, m1, k1. 31 sts.
Work 3 rows in st st.
Next row K13, k2 tog, k1, skpo, k13.
P 1 row.
Next row K12, k2 tog, k1, skpo, k12.
P 1 row. Cast off.
Join sole and back seam. With crochet hook, make two 10cm/4in long chain cords for ties. Attach one end of each cord to either side of shoe. Make one more.

Tutu

Fold net in half and gather folded edge, pull up to fit twice around bear's waist. Place on bear and secure in position.

Pilgrim Bears

See Pages
30/31

MATERIALS
Bear 3 25g hanks of Rowan Lightweight DK.
Small amount of Brown yarn for embroidery.
Pair of 2¾mm (No 12/US 2) knitting needles.
Stuffing.
Boys outfit 5 25g hanks of Rowan Lightweight DK in Black (A).
Small amount of same in Gold.
Small amount of Rowan Cotton Glace in White (B).
Pair each of 2¾mm (No 12/US 2 or 1), 3 mm (No 11/US 2) and 3¼mm (No 10/US 3) knitting needles.
Small size crochet hook.
4 buttons for jacket, 1 button for collar.
Length of shirring elastic.
Girls outfit 2 25g hanks of Rowan Lightweight DK in Black (A).
1 50g ball of Rowan Cotton Glace in White (B).

Pair each of 2¾mm (No 12/US 2 or 1), 3 mm (No 11/US 2) and 3¼mm (No 10/US 3) knitting needles.
Small size crochet hook.
3 buttons for dress, 1 button for collar.

MEASUREMENTS
Bear approximately 27cm/10½in high.

TENSIONS
32 sts and 40 rows to 10cm/4in square over st st using Lightweight DK yarn and 2¾mm (No 12/US 2) needles.
28 sts and 36 rows to 10cm/4in square over st st using Lightweight DK yarn and 3¼mm (No 10/US 3) needles.

ABBREVIATIONS
See page 5.

Bear

Work as given for Bear in Nightshirt with Hat (see page 35).

Jacket

BACK
With 3¼mm (No 10/US 3) needles and A, cast on 44 sts. K 3 rows.
Beg with a k row, work 18 rows in st st.
Change to 2¾mm (No 12/US 2) needles and work 4 rows.
Change to 3¼mm (No 10/US 3) needles and work 4 rows.
Shape Armholes
Cast off 3 sts at beg of next 2 rows. 38 sts. Work 16 rows straight.
Shape Shoulders
Cast off 11 sts at beg of next 2 rows.
Leave rem 16 sts on a holder.

LEFT FRONT
With 3¼mm (No 10/US 3) needles and A, cast on 23 sts. K 3 rows.
1st row K.
2nd row K3, p to end.
Rep last 2 rows 8 times more.
Change to 2¾mm (No 12/US 2) needles.
Buttonhole row K to last 4 sts, k2 tog, yf, k2.
Work 3 rows.

Change to 3¼mm (No 10/US 3) needles and work 4 rows.
Shape Armhole
Next row Cast off 3 sts, k to last 4 sts, k2 tog, yf, k2.
Work 7 rows. Rep the buttonhole row again. Work 4 rows.
Shape Neck
Next row K3 and slip these sts onto safety pin, p2 tog, p to end.
Dec one st at neck edge on next 5 rows.
11 sts. Work 3 rows. Cast off.

RIGHT FRONT
With 3¼mm (No 10/US 3) needles and A, cast on 23 sts. K 3 rows.
1st row K.
2nd row P to last 3 sts, k3.
Complete to match Left Front, omitting buttonholes.

SLEEVES
Join shoulder seams.
With 3¼mm (No 10/US 3) needles, A and right side facing, k up 44 sts along straight edge of armhole. P 1 row.
Next row K16, [k twice in next st] 12 times, k16. 56 sts.
Beg with a p row, work 11 rows in st st, dec one st at each end of 5 foll alt rows. 46 sts.
Next row K13, [k2 tog] 10 times, k13. 36 sts.
Change to 2¾mm (No 12/US 2) needles.

K 2 rows. Cast off.

NECKBAND
With 2¾mm (No 12/US 2) needles, A and right side facing, sl the 3 sts on right front safety pin onto needle, k up 13 sts up right front neck, k back neck sts dec one st at each end, k up 13 sts down left front neck, then k3 sts from safety pin. 46 sts. K 3 rows, making buttonhole at end of 2nd row as before. Cast off.

COLLAR
With 3¼mm (No 10/US 3) needles and B, cast on 64 sts.
Change to 3 mm (No 11/US 2) needles.
K 3 rows.
Next row K2, k2 tog, k to last 4 sts, skpo, k2.
Next row K2, p2 tog tbl, p to last 4 sts, p2 tog, k2.
Next row K2, k2 tog, k32, yf, sl 1, yb, turn.
Next row Sl 1, p12, yb, sl 1, yf, turn.
Next row Sl 1, k17, yf, sl 1, yb, turn.
Next row Sl 1, p22, yb, sl 1, yf, turn.
Next row Sl 1, k27, yf, sl 1, yb, turn.
Next row Sl 1, p32, yb, sl 1, yf, turn.
Next row Sl 1, k to last 4 sts, skpo, k2.
Change to 2¾mm (No 12/ US 1) needles.
Next row K2, p2 tog tbl, p to last 4 sts, p2 tog, k2.
Next row K2, k2 tog, k to last 4 sts, skpo, k2.
Next row K2, p2 tog tbl, p to last 4 sts, p2 tog, k2. 52 sts.
Next row K2, k2 tog, k15, [k2 tog] 7 times, k15, skpo, k2. 43 sts.
K 2 rows. Cast off.

CUFFS (MAKE 2)
With 2¾mm (No 12/US 2) needles and B, cast on 34 sts. K 3 rows.
Next row K2, k2 tog, k to last 4 sts, skpo, k2.
Next row K2, p2 tog tbl, p to last 4 sts, p2 tog, k2.
Rep last 2 rows once more. 26 sts. K2 rows. Cast off.

TO MAKE UP
Sew first 4 row end edges of sleeve tops to cast off sts at armholes. Join side and sleeve seams. Sew on buttons. With crochet hook, make buttonhole loop at top of one side of collar. Sew button to wrong side of other side of collar. Join cuff seams half way up from cast off edges. With crochet hook make chain 36cm/16in long for tie.

Breeches

TO MAKE
With 2¾mm (No 12/US 2) needles and A, cast on 36 sts for one leg. K3 rows. Change to 3¼mm (No 10/US 3) needles.
Next row K1, [k twice in next st, k3, k twice in next st, k2] to end. 46 sts.
Beg with a p row, work 9 rows in st st, inc one st at each end of every row. 64 sts.
Shape Crotch
Cast off 4 sts at beg of next 2 rows. 56 sts. Work 16 rows straight.
Next row K4, [k2 tog] 24 times, k4. 32 sts.
Change to 2¾mm (No 12/US 2) needles. K 2 rows. Cast off.
Make one more. Join all seams. Thread length of shirring elastic along wrong side of all garter st borders and fasten off.

Hat

TO MAKE
With 2¾mm (No 12/US 2) needles and using two strands of A yarn together, cast on 53 sts for brim. Beg with a k row, work 10 rows in st st.
Next row K1, [k2 tog, k11] 4 times. Work 3 rows.
Next row K1, [k2 tog, k10] 4 times. Work 3 rows.
Cont in this way, dec 4 sts as set on next row and 2 foll 4th rows. 33 sts. Work 3 rows. Cast off.
With 2¾mm (No 12/US 2) needles, right side facing and using two strands of A yarn together, k up 53 sts along cast on edge of brim.
Next row P4, [p twice in next st, p3] to last st, p1. 65 sts.
Beg with a k row, work 2 rows in st st.
Next row K1, [k twice in next st, k3] to end.
Work 2 rows.
Next row [P4, p twice in next st] to last st, p1. 97 sts.
Work 2 rows. Cast off purlwise.
With 2¾mm (No 12/US 2) needles and using two strands of A yarn together, cast on 5 sts for crown. Work in st st, inc one st at each end of 2nd row and foll row, then on foll alt row. 11 sts. Work 7 rows straight. Dec one st at each end of next row and foll alt row, then at each end of foll row. Cast off.
With 2¾mm (No 12/US 2) needles and using one strand of A yarn, cast on 5 sts for belt. K 126 rows.
Next row K2 tog, k1, k2 tog tbl.
K 1 row. Work 3 tog and fasten off.
With 2¾mm (No 12/US 2) needles and one strand of Gold yarn, cast on 10 sts for buckle. K 2 rows.
Next row K3, cast off 4, k to end.
Next row K3, cast on 4, k to end.
K 1 row. Rep last 3 rows once more. Cast off.
Join back seam of brim, then sew in crown. Sew cast on edge of belt to buckle. Place belt on hat and secure in position.

Dress

FRONT
With 3¼mm (No 10/US 3) needles and A, cast on 60 sts. K 3 rows. Beg with a k row, work 36 rows in st st.
Next row K2, [k2 tog, k2, k2 tog, k1] to last 2 sts, k2. 44 sts. **
Work 5 rows.
Shape Armholes
Cast off 3 sts at beg of next 2 rows. 38 sts. Work 12 rows straight.
Shape Neck
Next row K15, turn.
Work on this set of sts only. Dec one st at neck edge on next row and 3 foll alt rows. 11 sts. Work 2 rows. Cast off.
With right side facing, slip centre 8 sts onto a holder, rejoin yarn to rem sts and k to end. Complete to match first side.

BACK
Work as given for Front to **. Work 2 rows.
Divide for Opening
Next row P20, k3, turn.
Work on this set of sts only. Keeping the 3 sts at inside edge in garter st (every row k) and remainder in st st, work 3 rows.
Shape Armhole
Cast off 3 sts at beg of next row. 20 sts. Work 16 rows straight.
Shape Neck
Next row K3 and slip these sts onto a safety pin, k to end.
Dec one st at neck edge on next 6 rows. 11 sts. Cast off.
With wrong side facing, rejoin yarn to rem sts, cast on 2, k3, p to end. Complete to match first side, working buttonholes on 3rd and 13th rows as follows:
Buttonhole row (right side) K to last 4 sts, k2 tog, yf, k2.

SLEEVES
Join shoulder seams.
With 3¼mm (No 10/US 3) needles and A, k up and k44 sts along straight edge of armhole. P 1 row.
Next row K16, [k twice in next st] 12 times, k16. 56 sts.
Beg with a p row, work 12 rows in st st,

dec one st at each end of 6 foll alt rows. 44 sts. Work 1 row.
Next row K14, [k2 tog] 8 times, k14. 36 sts. Change to 2¾mm (No 12/US 2) needles. K 2 rows. Cast off.

NECKBAND
With 2¾mm (No 12/US 2) needles, A and right side facing, slip the 3 sts from left back safety pin onto needle, k up 9 sts up left back neck, 12 sts down left front neck, k centre front sts, k up 12 sts up right front neck and 9 sts down right back neck, k3 sts from safety pin. 56 sts. K 3 rows, making buttonhole at end of 2nd row. Cast off.

COLLAR, CUFFS AND TO MAKE UP
Work as given for Collar, Cuffs and To Make Up of Jacket, omitting making tie.

Apron

TO MAKE
With 3¼mm (No 10/US 3) needles and B, cast on 22 sts. K 3 rows.
Next row K.
Next row K2, p18, k2.
Rep last 2 rows 11 times more.
Change to 2¾mm (No 12/US 2) needles.
Next row Cast on 50 sts, k57, [k2 tog] 4 times, k7.
Next row Cast on 50 sts, k to end. Cast off.

Cap

TO MAKE
With 3¼mm (No 10/US 3) needles and B, cast on 25 sts for brim.
Next row K9, p16.
Next row K16, p7, k2.
Work 18 rows. Mark beg of last row.
Work 21 rows. Mark end of last row.
Work 20 rows. Cast off.
With 3¼mm (No 10/US 3) needles and B, cast on 14 sts for crown. P 1 row.
Next row K1, [k twice in next st] to last st, k1. 26 sts.
Beg with a p row, work 19 rows in st st.
Next row K1, [k2 tog] to last st, k1. 14 sts. Cast off.
Placing cast off edge of crown between markers of brim, sew in crown. Form 3 stitch pleat around the seam just worked and slip stitch in position.
With 3¼mm (No 10/US 3) needles and B, cast on 40 sts, then k up 33 sts along lower edge of cap, omitting first and last 9 sts, cast on 40 sts. 113 sts. K 2 rows. Cast off. Turn back first 9 sts of brim.

Rugby Bear

See Page
32

MATERIALS

Bear 3 25g hanks of Rowan Lightweight DK.
Small amount of Brown yarn for embroidery.
Pair of 2¾mm (No 12/US 2) knitting needles.
Stuffing.
Outfit 1 50g ball of Rowan DK Handknit Cotton in each of 3 contrasting colours A, B and C.
Pair each of 3¼mm (No 10/US 3) and 4 mm (No 8/US 6) knitting needles.
2 buttons.

MEASUREMENTS

Bear approximately 27cm/10½in high.

TENSIONS

32 sts and 40 rows to 10cm/4in square over st st using Lightweight DK yarn and 2¾mm (No 12/US 2) needles.
20 sts and 28 rows to 10cm/4in square over st st using DK Handknit yarn and 4 mm (No 8/US 6) needles.

ABBREVIATIONS

See page 5.

Bear

Work as given for Bear in Nightshirt with Hat (see page 35).

Shirt

FRONT

With 3¼mm (No 10/US 3) needles and A, cast on 24 sts. K 3 rows.
Change to 4 mm (No 8/US 6) needles.
Next row K.
Next row K2, p20, k2.
Rep last 2 rows once more. Beg with a k row, work 2 rows in st st across all sts.
Cont in st st and stripe patt of 6 rows B and 6 rows A throughout, work 16 rows.
Divide for Opening
Next row Patt 10, k3C, turn.

Work on this set of sts only, twisting yarns together on wrong side when changing colour to avoid holes.
Next row K3C, patt to end.
Keeping the 3 sts at inside edge in C and garter st (every row k) and remainder in st st and stripe patt, work 2 rows.
Buttonhole row Patt 10, with C, k2 tog, yf, k1.
Work 9 rows, then rep the buttonhole row again.
Shape Neck
Cast off 3 sts at beg of next row. Dec one st at neck edge on next 4 rows. 6 sts. Patt 3 rows. Break off yarn.
With right side facing, rejoin yarn to rem 11 sts, cast on 2 sts, k to end.
Next row Patt 10, k3.
Next row K3, patt to end.
Rep last 2 rows 5 times more, then work

first of the 2 rows again.
Shape Neck
Cast off 3 sts at beg of next row. Dec one st at neck edge on next 4 rows. 6 sts. Patt 4 rows.

BACK

Next row Patt to end, cast on 12 sts, patt across first set of sts. 24 sts.
Patt 40 rows.
Next row P2, patt 20, p2.
Rep last row 3 times more.
Change to 3¼mm (No 10/US 3) needles.
With A, p2 rows. Cast off.

SLEEVES

With 4 mm (No 8/US 6) needles, A and right side facing, k up 34 sts between beginning of 5th stripe on Front and Back. Beg with a p row, work in st st and stripe patt of 5 rows A, 6 rows B and 6 rows A, **at the same time**, dec one st at each end of 5th row and 3 foll 4th rows. 26 sts.
Change to 3¼mm (No 10/US 3) needles.
With C, k 3 rows. Cast off.

COLLAR

With 3¼mm (No 10/US 3) needles, C, right side facing and beginning and ending 3 sts in from front edge, k up 41 sts around neck edge. K 9 rows. Cast off loosely.

TO MAKE UP

Join sleeve seams, then side seams to top of side edge borders. Sew on buttons.

Yarn Source Guide

Rowan Yarn Addresses
Rowan Yarns are widely available in yarn shops. For details of stockists and mail order sources of Rowan Yarns, please write or contact the distributors listed below.
For advice on how to use a substitute yarn, see page 5.

UNITED KINGDOM
Rowan Yarns,
Green Lane Mill, Holmfirth,
West Yorkshire, England
HD7 1RW
Tel: (01484) 681 881

USA
Westminster Trading Corporation,
5 Northern Boulevard, Amherst,
NH 03031
Tel: (603) 886 5041/5043

AUSTRALIA
Rowan (Australia),
191 Canterbury Road,
Canterbury, Victoria 3126
Tel: (03) 830 1609

BELGIUM
Hedera,
Pleinstraat 68,
3001 Leuven
Tel: (016) 23 21 89

CANADA
Estelle Designs & Sales Ltd,
Unit 65 & 67, 2220 Midland Avenue,
Scarborough, Ontario, M10 3E6
Tel: (416) 298 9922

DENMARK
Designer Garn,
Vesterbro 33 A,
DK-9000, Aalborg
Tel: (8) 98 13 48 24

FRANCE
Elle Tricote,
52 Rue Principale,
67300 Schiltigheim
Tel: (33) 88 62 65 31

GERMANY
Wolle + Design,
Wolfshover Strasse 76,
52428 Julich Stetternich
Tel: (49) 2461 54735

HOLLAND
Henk & Henrietta Beukers,
Dorpsstraat 9,
NL 5327 AR Hurwenen
Tel: (04182) 1764

ICELAND
Stockurinn,
Kjorgardi, Laugavegi 59,
ICE-101 Reykjavik
Tel: (01) 18254

ITALY
La Compagnia del Cotone,
Via Mazzini 44, I-10123 Torino
Tel: (011) 87 83 81

JAPAN
Diakeito Co Ltd,
2-3-11 Senba-Higashi, Minoh City,
Osaka 562
Tel: (0727) 27 6604

NEW ZEALAND
John Q Goldingham Ltd,
PO Box 45083, Epuni Railway,
Lower Hutt, Wellington, North Island
Tel: (04) 5674 085

NORWAY
Eureka,
PO Box 357, N-1401 Ski
Tel: (64) 86 55 70

SWEDEN
Wincent,
Sveavagen 94,
113 58 Stockholm
Tel: (08) 673 70 60

Author's Acknowledgments

I would like to thank my knitters, Maisie Lawrence and Frances Wallace for their patience and hard work. I am particularly grateful to Sandra Lane for her beautiful photography, and Marie Willey for her excellent styling and propping.

I would also like to thank Denise Bates for making this project possible, Clare Johnson and, as always, my agent Heather Jeeves for doing such a brilliant job.